Chicken Chores
AND Open Doors

Paul learns to walk with God

ISBN: 978-1-936208-62-3

Illustrations: Jerron Hess
Cover design: Teresa Sommers
Layout: Felicia Kern

Printed January 2012
Printed in the USA

For more information about Christian Aid Ministries, see page 167.

Published by:
TGS International
P.O. Box 355
Berlin, Ohio 44610 USA
Phone: 330·893·4828
Fax: 330·893·2305
www.tgsinternational.com

TGS00453

Chicken Chores
AND Open Doors

Paul learns to walk with God

JULIA STAUFFER

Conestoga Bookstore
2175 Division Highway
Ephrata, PA   17522-8967
717-354-0475

Acknowledgments
and Thanks to:

- God, who brought me from death unto life. I write because of His inspiration. May He receive all glory and honor.

- Lawrence, my beloved husband, who offered much encouragement.

- Isaiah, Drew, and Adam: May you grow up to serve the Lord like Grandpa!

- Dad, for the many phone calls, verifications, and insights.

- Friends and family who showed an interest and encouraged me to write.

Table of Contents

Introduction

Paul Weaver and his family lived on a farm among the rolling hills of Holmes County, Ohio. Paul's dad's name was Raymond, and his mom's name was Lizzie Ann. Paul had two sisters, Esther and Mary, and four brothers: Wayne, Jake, Roy, and John. Paul and his family were Amish. They drove a horse and buggy instead of a car, and the children walked almost a mile to school every day.

Dad was a preacher in the Amish church and a schoolteacher at South Bunker Hill School. He also had a chicken house that held ten thousand chickens. Paul and his family were very busy. Paul and his brothers always had chores to do, ponies to ride, things to repair, sisters to tease, balls to hit, and minnows to catch in the little creek that ran through their farm.

Being Amish meant more to Paul and his family than just dressing a certain way and living a simple life. Being Amish also meant living in obedience to

God and His Word, the Bible. Dad believed that "in order to die right a person needs to live right," so every night by the glow of the gas lantern, the whole family would listen as Dad read stories from the Bible. He also taught about what God wants people to do: be born again, be honest, and most of all, love God with all their hearts.

Paul's family followed Amish traditions such as having a good work ethic and keeping a slower-paced life. The family also believed in sharing each other's burdens. If one of the other families in the church had a house fire or a high medical bill, all the people in the church would find out about it and help with the expense.

Paul's family, like all other Amish families, believed that there is more evil than good shown on television, so they chose not to have television or other modern entertainments in their home. Their evenings were spent doing things like swinging on the porch swing, singing, and playing ball or hide-and-go-seek. They felt these were more worthwhile activities than sitting in front of a television.

Unfortunately, many Amish homes don't have the teaching Paul received. Those who have not been born again find themselves enslaved to wrong habits, even though they attend the Amish church. The lifestyles of some unsaved Amish people have given the world the idea that all Amish have similar lifestyles. Even though this is not true, it has sadly damaged the testimony of this group of Anabaptist people.

The stories in this book tell of lessons Paul

learned in his growing-up years and adulthood. These lessons impacted the rest of his life as well as the lives of many other people who have heard the stories. May God be glorified!

Note: The names of some people in this book have been changed to protect their identity.

Part One:
Obeying God

Chapter 1
A Snake and the Truth

"A false witness shall not be unpunished,
and he that speaketh lies shall not escape."
—Proverbs 19:5

The heat seemed almost unbearable in the little one-room schoolhouse. When Teacher Effie finally announced dismissal, all the students rushed madly out the door. Paul worked the long handle of the water pump, and soon fresh, cold water gushed out. The younger boys pushed and shoved as they waited their turn in the line. It seemed that the bigger you were, the faster you got anything you wanted. Right now everyone wanted a drink.

Although it was hot and the autumn breeze was nowhere to be found, it was still a wonderful time of year. It had been a good day of school for Paul and his siblings, Esther and Wayne. Esther ran over to where Paul was chatting with his friends. "Paul, come on. We need to get going. You know what Mom said. She wants us to come home right after school."

"Ach, Esther," Paul rolled his eyes. "What's the hurry? I suppose you want to go home and clean up the garden for Mom?"

"Oh, you!" Esther retorted. Paul knew she hated pulling weeds and often reminded her of it.

"Besides, I'm too hot to start off right now," Paul said, sitting down in the shade of a nearby tree. His friends chuckled as they watched Esther stomp off toward the schoolhouse.

"She sure bosses me around," Paul said with a grin, tossing his hat up in the air and catching it on his finger. He sighed and laid his hat beside him in the grass. Paul's younger brother Wayne ran up and joined in the chatter and laughter.

A short while later Esther peered around the coal shed and motioned for Paul to come. "Well, I may as well succumb to Miss Bossy," Paul announced, and the little huddle dispersed as they all started off toward home.

The boys took the lead on the walk home, laughing, pushing each other into the ditch, and tussling as they went. The girls followed more sedately, whispering to each other about how the boys acted just like barnyard roosters: puffing out their chests, strutting proudly, and acting as though they didn't know the girls were watching. Oh, such silly boys!

The little group had walked only a little way down the road when the boys spotted a truck stopped beside the road.

"Hmm, I wonder what's going on," Paul thought out loud.

"That's a Ford for you, always clunking out!" exclaimed Danny. "They're not near as steady as our horse, Sam." Danny sounded so sure of his words that no one dared disagree.

Esther surveyed the truck and, as the oldest child present, took her responsibility seriously. "Come here, boys," she said. They all stood around Esther, looking at the truck while Esther pointed out some of the dangers associated with a stopped truck. The boys weren't very concerned and started snickering. Esther reprimanded them. "Boys, shh, I think I see a man sleeping in the truck, so don't be loud! He might be a bad man. Who knows?"

The boys were not deterred from their foolishness in the least, and Esther shook her head in disgust as the boys continued their way home. Alvin tripped over his own feet and went sliding into the ditch. Paul and Danny held their hands over their mouths and keeled over with laughter. The girls found Alvin's antics neither amusing nor comical and quickly tried to distance themselves from the boys and their clamor. The boys picked up their feet a little higher and were more careful as they got close to the truck.

After the girls had passed the truck without waking the man, Esther sighed with relief. She glanced at the other girls and nodded her head in satisfaction. Then out of the corner of her eye she saw something that made her shudder with fear—a dead snake! It lay beside the road where it had been hit, its head smashed and bits of skin torn off. The boys came over to where the dead snake lay, about twenty yards past the stopped truck.

"Ahh, I have a brilliant idea," Paul said, picking up the snake and grinning at Esther to see her

reaction. He got the exact response he hoped to see.

"Don't you dare, Paul!" Esther whispered as loud as she dared. "Don't you dare throw it at me or I'll scream and wake up that man!"

Paul chuckled. "I wasn't going to throw it at you. I have a much better plan." With that he strode back to the truck.

Esther's eyes opened wide and she clamped her hand over her mouth. She turned and ran for home with the other girls in tow. She glanced back only once, just in time to see Paul fling the snake into the truck's open window. The horrified girl ran home as fast as she could, her feet fairly flying down the last hill. She didn't even stop to say goodbye to her friends; instead, she ran up the driveway and sped straight to Dad's shop in the basement of the house. Esther burst into the shop to find Dad there, whistling while he worked, as he often did in the afternoons. Dad jumped. "What is going on with my Sally Mae?" he teased.

Esther gave him the whole tale, starting with Paul not obeying Mom by loitering after school, telling how he was careless around the stopped truck, and ending with the awful story about the snake.

"Hmm," Dad replied with a furrowed brow. "Don't worry, Esther, I'll take care of it. Thank you for telling me."

"I think Paul should have a hard spanking!" Esther declared with her hands planted firmly on her hips.

"I said I'll take care of it," Dad said firmly. "Now

run along and help your mom."

"Okay," Esther replied. She turned and ran upstairs.

The boys also had watched Paul pick up the snake. After he had thrown it into the truck, all three boys turned and ran away.

Danny and Alvin really did admire Paul's boldness and they enjoyed the fun, but they felt mightily relieved they didn't have to do anything with the snake themselves.

When they topped the last hill, Paul sighed with relief. The truck driver hadn't woken up. Paul started feeling proud of his accomplishment. He chuckled and said, "Won't that driver be surprised to find a dead snake in his truck?"

"Sure will!" Danny replied, slapping his knee. The boys roared with laughter.

"It'll be a wonderful story in school tomorrow too!" Paul said with a smirk.

"That's for sure!" Alvin grinned, nodding his head.

By now they had reached Paul's home. Paul waved goodbye to his friends and headed in the lane. He left his lunch box on the lawn and went to the chicken house. There he scooped up a baby chick and brushed his cheek against its soft yellow down. Only yesterday the shipment of ten thousand chicks had come, and it was one of Paul's favorite pastimes to hold and cuddle the little peepers. He sat down in the sawdust and let the chicks peck at his shoes. After a while he stood up and made his way back to the door, careful not to step on the little chicks as they scattered with soft protests and fluttering little wings.

Paul opened the door and skipped across the lawn. Picking up his lunch box, he glanced toward the house just in time to see Wayne rounding the corner of the house, his cheeks bulging and a cinnamon roll in his hand.

"Did Mom give you that?" Paul asked, surprised.

"Uh-huh," Wayne said as he took another bite.

That was all Paul needed to know. He grabbed his lunch box and ran into the house.

"Hi, sonny boy," Mom said cheerfully. "Would you like to sample a roll?"

"May I?"

"Under one condition: you go down to the fruit cellar and get me two quarts of canned beef so I can start supper soon."

"I'll do it."

"Okay, but mind now, don't forget!" Mom said, handing Paul his cinnamon roll.

Paul headed downstairs and almost ran into Dad on his way to the fruit cellar. "Hi, Dad," he grinned as he held up his cinnamon roll.

"Welcome home," Dad replied. "I think I'm going to have to find the cook who makes those rolls, but first, I need to talk to you!"

"What for, Dad?"

"I heard that someone by the name of Paul threw a snake into the open window of a truck. Was that you?"

"No! Wasn't me, Dad."

"You're sure?"

"Yes!" Paul took another bite. "I did pick up the

snake though, to scare Esther a bit."

"Well," Raymond eyed his son, "you shouldn't have done that either."

"I know."

"Paul, are you really telling me the truth?"

Paul fidgeted a little but firmly replied, "Yes!"

"Hmm," Dad said thoughtfully. "I need to go to town before long, but before I go, I want to talk with you some more. Right now I need to find a cinnamon roll." Dad turned and climbed the stairs.

A tinge of guilt swept over Paul as he stepped into the dark cellar to get the two jars of beef. He knew better! *Why do I talk faster than I think?* he wondered, upset that he had lied again. It was becoming easier and easier to lie. At first he had felt terribly guilty, but recently it didn't bother him as much unless he was caught in his lie. Just now, though, Paul felt awful. He didn't want to talk to Dad.

Paul opened the screen door just in time to hear Dad talking to Mom, "Well, *Frau*, I need to run to town to get some bolts and a belt. I'll be back soon. Sound okay with you?"

"Yes, would you be able to get some brown sugar for me?"

"I think that could be done," Raymond smiled at his wife. "How much?"

"Ten pounds," Lizzie Ann answered as she scoured the last of the dishes.

Paul placed the beef on the table and had turned to leave when Dad said, "Paul, come in to the bedroom."

Paul reluctantly obeyed. The weight of his sin pressed on his heart.

Dad closed the door behind his son and turned to address him. "Paul, I want you to sit down right here and tell me everything that happened on your way home from school today."

Paul knew he needed to confess his wrong, but oh, it was so hard. Finally he told the whole story. He could see Dad was disappointed in him, and Paul truly was sorry he had lied. He hung his head in shame as Dad reached for a wooden paddle he kept in the bedroom. Dad called it his rod of correction.

After the spanking, Paul quieted his sobs and wiped his eyes. He was still sniffling when Dad said, "You always need to remember, Paul, that a lie is something God hates. And throwing a snake into a truck was a very bad witness. God commands us to do unto others as we would want them to treat us. The reason I had to spank you was so you remember to obey and never tell a lie. Can I depend on you to be more loving and truthful?"

"Yes." Paul looked up into his dad's kind eyes.

"You know I love you, don't you?" Dad asked, giving Paul a tight hug.

"Yeah."

"Good! Now I have an assignment for you. I want you to memorize a verse in the Bible, and when I get home from town, I want you to say it to me." Dad reached for his Bible and turned to Proverbs 19:5. "It says here, 'A false witness shall not be unpunished, and he that speaketh lies shall not escape.' " Dad handed the Bible to Paul and pointed out the verse. Then Dad left for town.

Paul took the Bible outside to the wooden porch swing. He said the verse to himself again and again and again. But then his thoughts started wandering to the neighbors, his rabbits, his pony, and cinnamon rolls. Then he remembered the verse and studied it again.

After Paul was confident he could say the verse, he jumped off the swing and ran off in search of Wayne. Paul found him playing with his homemade drilling rig in the pasture, but Paul didn't feel like drilling for water. He took his favorite rabbit out of the pen and sat down in the shade to think. True, his pride had been hurt, but he felt a lot better since he told Dad the truth. Paul actually felt bad for the poor trucker who would wake up to find a nasty-looking snake in his cab.

Soon Betty the horse came trotting in the lane, pulling Dad's buggy behind her. Paul stood up and walked over to the hitching post with his rabbit nestled in his arms. "Hi, son," Dad called out. "Did you learn your verse?"

"Yes, I did," Paul replied.

"Can you say it to me?"

Paul furrowed his brow, thought a moment, and recited out loud, "A false witness shall not be unpunished, and he that speaketh lies shall not escape."

Dad smiled and said, "Good, son, very good! Now remember that verse. Whenever you're tempted to tell a lie, always remember you will be punished for it either here on earth or at Judgment Day. I want you to pray now and ask God to forgive you for lying and for being a bad testimony."

Paul and Dad bowed their heads and Paul prayed, "God, I'm sorry I lied and was a bad testimony when I threw the snake inside the truck. Please forgive me and help me not to lie again. Amen."

Dad opened his eyes and said, "All right, run along now and see if Mom has any jobs for you today."

Paul carefully dropped his rabbit back into the pen and skipped back to the house. His heart felt as light as a feather. The sorrow of sin no longer held him tight. And Paul never forgot the lesson he learned: he must always tell the truth.

Chapter 2
"I'm Not Going to Church!"

"Children, obey your parents in the Lord: for this is right."
—Ephesians 6:1

Lizzie Ann scurried around the kitchen, thinking faster than she worked. *Hmm, I need a sippy cup for Mary, a cup of pretzels for Roy, and . . . oh, I need to wake the children.* She hurried over to the broom closet. Grabbing the broom, she went to the wood stove and used the broom handle to pound on the tin chimney pipe that conveniently ran up through Paul's room. *Bang! Bang! Bang!* "Yooo-hooo," she called. "Wake up, children. Time to get ready for church."

No answer. Lizzie Ann banged again, this time a little harder and a lot louder. *BANG! BANG! BANG!*

"Yeah," Paul shouted from his spot beneath the covers. He knew Mom wouldn't stop that awful racket until someone woke up and hollered. Sure enough, the banging stopped, and Mom went back to scurrying about the kitchen.

Paul lay in bed looking up at the ceiling. *Oh no,* he groaned to himself, *today's Sunday, and Dad has to preach in a different church.* Paul's dad was sometimes asked to preach in neighboring Amish churches, and Paul always dreaded the strangers he would have to meet. He rolled over and tried to go back to sleep. Dreaming about a Sunday in a strange church would be a lot better than actually being there.

Ten minutes later, there were more bangs. This time Mom hit the chimney so hard that Paul bolted out of bed and called, "I'm coming!" He hurried downstairs for breakfast.

Mom was busy cooking oatmeal when Paul came down into the kitchen. "Good morning, sonny boy," she said. "It's about time you shake off your sleep. Here, have a bite of oatmeal." She set a bowl on the table for Paul.

Esther, Wayne, and Jake were already scraping up the last of their oatmeal. Apparently they weren't dreading going to church like Paul was.

Paul sat down just as Dad came into the room. Dad ruffled Paul's and Wayne's hair and addressed them all. "We've got to leave in about an hour, and Paul, I want you to feed the chickens before we go."

"But Dad, I don't want to go to a strange church. The people always stare at me. They're not even nice," Paul said grumpily.

"Paul, that is no way to talk. You know those people have good hearts. Maybe you're just imagining things. They don't look at you that much," Dad reassured. "Think of me. I stand up there preaching, and yes, everyone is watching me, but that's okay. I know they're listening."

"Do you want to know something else?" Paul asked sadly. "They're always picking on me because I'm so short, and I get so tired of it!" Paul was short for his age, and on occasions like this it really bothered him.

"Well, Paul, I've got to go study just a little bit more. I want you to go with us without complaining. Think of what Jesus would want you to do." With that, Dad went out of the room and Paul was left to his thoughts. Oh, he didn't want to go! His oatmeal was starting to taste like glue. It got caught in his throat and almost choked him when he thought about going to church. Paul coughed.

Mom's voice interrupted his thoughts. "Paul, now hurry up. Finish that oatmeal. You'll need to hurry to feed those chickens. We don't want to wait on you."

Paul finished his oatmeal and got up from his chair, but instead of going upstairs to change into his Sunday clothes, he tiptoed to the screen door leading to the front porch. Quietly he unlatched it and stepped into the fresh morning air.

Outside, the soft fog was slowly lifting to reveal the hue of the morning sky. The surrounding fields glistened with dew. The sun's rays were stretching themselves across heavy heads of golden wheat. It was a beautiful morning. Paul sighed as he took in all the details. *Oh, if I could stay home, I'd have all kinds of things to do! I'd climb the big maple tree and dangle my legs in the breeze.* Just the thought of it made Paul want to run out and shinny up the big tree. It was one of his favorite spots on the

18

homestead—after his place at the kitchen table, of course.

Paul thought of what Dad had just said: "What do you think Jesus would want you to do?" A wave of rebellion rose up inside Paul. *I'm not going to church!* he decided defiantly. *I've gone to church for years; I don't see why I couldn't miss this once.* Paul leaned his small frame over the porch railing. *God will understand. He won't care,* Paul assured himself. Idly, he reached out and pulled at a long strand of shrubbery growing along the railing.

In that instant, something caught the corner of his eye. Paul jerked erect. His mouth fell open, and fear clutched at his heart. There in front of the maple tree shone a dazzling white being. It stood quietly just a few feet from Paul and gazed directly at him. Paul stood rooted to the spot. *Why, it must be an angel!* he thought. Paul couldn't believe his eyes. His heart throbbed so hard that his whole body shook.

The angel had wings that shone. His hands were folded just like Mom's when she prayed. Everything about him was brilliant white: his robe, his wings, his hair, and his face. There was something about his eyes . . . a piercing sobriety that made Paul uncomfortable. The angel didn't say a word to explain why he had come, but Paul knew the reason.

Finally, Paul gathered enough courage to move. He turned and ran into the house, the screen door slamming behind him. Mom was just drying her hands on a tea towel when she turned to see Paul bursting into the kitchen, his eyes wide with fright. "Mom, come quick—an angel!"

"What?" Mom exclaimed, running across the kitchen and out to the porch. They looked toward the maple tree, but the angel was nowhere to be seen.

"He's gone!" Paul said in wonder. "He was standing right over there. I saw him!"

"Hmm." Mom studied the area. "Isn't that something!"

"Yes, and my heart is still pounding really hard," Paul said with his hand on his chest.

"Well, my boy," Mom said, "That is the most amazing thing! I'm sure God is trying to tell you something!"

"I know," Paul soberly replied.

Entering the kitchen, Raymond heard his wife and Paul talking excitedly on the front porch. Raymond came out to the porch and Paul rushed over to him. "Daddy, I just saw an angel! He was right over there." Paul pointed to the maple tree.

Dad's mouth dropped open a little in disbelief. "Really?"

"Yes!"

"Did he tell you something?" Dad asked, staring out toward the tree.

"No, he didn't; he just looked at me," Paul replied.

Dad gently put his hand on Paul's shoulder and said, "Paul, don't you think that God sent that angel to tell you how important it is to go to church?"

Paul hung his head in shame and murmured, "Yes. I'm sorry I didn't want to go." He swiped at the mist in his eyes.

They all stood quietly for a brief moment, pondering the ways of God. Then Mom said, "Well, now that you want to go to church, you'd better hurry upstairs and get ready."

"Yes," Dad agreed. "I have Betty harnessed, and we need to leave in ten minutes."

Paul bounded upstairs. As he stood in his room buttoning his crisp white shirt, he heard his mom and dad talking about what he had just seen. Their voices were filled with awe. Paul himself was filled with wonder all over. He breathed a prayer. "God, I'm so sorry for not wanting to go to church. From now on, I'll always go to church without complaining!"

The house was quiet as Paul quickly combed his hair and splashed some cold water on his face at the washbasin. Everyone was waiting on him when he got outside to the buggy. Paul jumped up, Dad helped him over the seat, and they were on their way.

All the way to church, God kept speaking to Paul's heart, and by the time Betty rounded the bend at Jonas' place, Paul was firmly convinced that for the rest of his life he would always go to church wherever he was.

Yes, Paul went to church that Sunday and many Sundays after that. He and his family visited many different churches. Sometimes Paul was teased and even mocked, but that didn't keep him from going to church. He always remembered the lesson he learned from a bright angel on that long-ago Sunday.

Chapter 3
Digesting Candy Bars

"Thou shalt not steal."
—Exodus 20:15

One beautiful afternoon Paul sat in the shade of the chicken house, holding a baby chick and watching it peck at some feed he held in his hand. Paul could see Wayne and Mary as they played with Daffy, their little Boston Terrier pup. Wayne ran toward the barn with Daffy at his heels, and Mary came up from behind and tried to pull his tail. Daffy spun around, nipped at Mary's hands, rolled over, and chased his tail until he became so dizzy he had to stop. Then the puppy flopped down and rested his head on his paws. Soon Wayne started running again, and the whole scene repeated itself. Daffy was so cute! Wayne and Mary loved playing with him.

Paul put the chick back in the chicken house and ambled across the lane. *Hmm,* he thought to himself, *if only I had something sweet . . . something chocolaty, crunchy, and delicious. A candy bar would be the ticket!* Just thinking about a candy bar made his mouth water. *Oh well, maybe if I'd drink some water, it would take care of my sweet tooth.* Paul lazily walked up to the hydrant and lifted his face to the fresh, cold water, but to his disappointment, the water didn't satisfy his cravings. Then out of the corner of his eye, Paul saw movement in the direction of the road. He looked up to see Danny and Alvin, his friends and next-door neighbors, motioning him to join them.

Water still dripping off his chin, Paul skipped over to the edge of the road, just beyond his favorite maple tree.

"Want to come over and ride our pony?" Alvin called across the road.

Paul didn't have time to reply. "Naw," Danny interrupted, shaking his head. "We did that yesterday. Let's go down to the creek and catch crayfish."

"Ach, who feels like catching pop-eyed crays?" disagreed Alvin.

"All I feel like doing right now," Paul said, "is stuffing my belly full of candy bars."

"Oh, that sounds like a winner!" Danny said. "I know how we could get some."

"Really?" Paul raised his eyebrows. "How?"

"Why don't you go ask your mom if you may come over, and I'll take care of the rest?" Danny suggested.

"It's a deal," Paul said as he turned to make his way to the top of the cellar steps. He knew Mom was down there, busy filling her fruit cellar shelves with the jars of peaches she had canned the day before.

Paul cupped his hands together and hollered

down the steps, "Mom!"

There was a long silence. "Yeah?" came the muffled reply from deep in the fruit cellar.

"May I go to Danny and Alvin's house to play for a while?" Paul asked, sitting down on the top step.

"Did you finish your homework?" Mom questioned as she came over to the door of the fruit cellar.

"Oh, yes! I only had two pages, you know." Paul was relieved Mom couldn't use that as a reason to refuse.

"Well, I suppose you may, for one hour, but mind now, be good."

"Yeah, Mom," Paul replied, jumping up excitedly. He ran until he reached the road. He stopped, looked both ways, and finally clambered up the bank on the opposite side of the road. Danny and Alvin clapped with excitement when they saw him. Paul stood puffing as Danny gave the orders.

"Okay, Paul, you and Alvin go into the silo and wait. I'll go get some candy from Dad's store. It might take a while, but you just wait until I come back." Danny and Alvin's dad, Joe, kept a variety of candy bars for sale in a special display case in his harness shop beside the barn.

Alvin and Paul ran toward the big red barn. As they walked through the open door into the shadowy barn, a sparrow suddenly fluttered out past them. Alvin jumped. "That almost hit me! What was it?"

Paul laughed. "Just a sparrow. Nothing worth jumping about."

The two boys quickly shinnied up the wooden ladder into the haymow. Next they climbed up a smaller ladder against the base of the silo. Then came the challenge. They had to open the door going into the silo while standing on the slanted chute. It took some persistent tugging until the silo door finally opened. Even the door seemed to squeak "candy" as it opened. Paul smiled to himself as he scrambled into the silo and onto the fresh mounds of silage.

"Can't see a thing," Alvin complained, bumping into the wall. His words echoed around them.

The inside of the silo seemed a bit eerie until their eyes adjusted to the low lighting. They heard a faint scurrying nearby. "What was that?" Alvin whispered, trying to be brave.

"Probably a rat," Paul answered. "My mom would say your nerves are bent out of shape."

The two boys waited a while. Paul was beginning to feel a bit uneasy himself as he dug his toes into the green silage.

Joe was busy cutting leather when Danny sneaked into the store. Quickly Danny ducked and grabbed two handfuls of the candy bars that were carefully arranged in the glass case in front of the counter. Turning, he bent at the waist so his dad couldn't see him sneaking away. Danny pushed the screen door open just wide enough to squeeze through and ran toward the protection of the barn.

Upon reaching the barn, Danny looked back through the shop window. He could see his dad bending over the leather. *Whew! Dad's still cutting*, he thought, relieved. Danny scrambled up the first ladder. Next he climbed the little ladder and

clattered up the silo chute. Alvin and Paul jumped in unison as Danny crawled into the silo with a twinkle in his eyes.

Paul let out a whistle. "We thought you'd never come."

"What took you so long?" Alvin asked, reaching for the candy bar Danny extended to him.

"You just thought it took long. It only took me a minute or two and Dad didn't see me at all. Can't get much better than that." Danny took a big bite of an Oh Henry! bar and added, "All I can say is, it sure was worth it!"

"Sure wush," Paul agreed through the big bite of candy bar bulging in his cheek.

"Uh-huh," grunted Alvin, his mouth too full for much comment.

Oh Henry!s and Paydays disappeared one by one into the mouths of the three boys. At last Paul stretched, rubbed his stomach, and said, "My sweet tooth feels much better, and my belly is satisfied with all that sugar!" He grinned and checked the rusty watch he kept in his pocket. "Looks like I can play for a half hour yet before I need to go home." With that the three boys made their way down the chute. Behind them lay the glimmering wrappers for some rodent to use for wallpaper or perhaps for a silky bed.

xxxxx

Danny thought they could swing from the old rope swing in the barn, but as usual Alvin wanted something more exciting and adventurous. Then

Paul suggested, "Why don't we ride Patsy and Speedy a while and play Indians?"

"Yeah, let's! We'll go get Speedy," cried Danny. As Danny ran for the small paddock where Speedy was grazing, Paul hurried across the road and around the house in search of Patsy.

Patsy was Paul's pony. She was a portly black pony with a white star on her forehead. She wasn't the fastest pony around, but Paul still loved her.

It was because of poky Patsy that Danny had named their pony Speedy. Speedy won every race in the neighborhood, mostly because he wasn't carrying as much weight around as the other ponies were. He was slim and snappy. Speedy held his head with pride as he galloped across the fields, while poor Patsy heaved and sighed at a trot. Speedy was a sorrel: a light brown body with a dark brown mane and tail. Everyone admitted he was a beauty. Because of Speedy, Danny and Alvin were the envy of all the schoolboys.

And so it was that Danny and Alvin jumped on Speedy, and Paul teamed with Patsy. The boys all rode bareback, legs hugging their mounts in a vise grip. Whooping and hollering, they kicked the flanks of their ponies and bounded off.

They crossed the meadow and entered a little wood where a teepee of sticks marked their camp. The boys tied the ponies to a tree and sat down to plan their adventure. Details settled, they set off on a buffalo hunt. Silently they snuck across a knoll and, topping it, saw a herd of cows on the other side. With yells and waves the boys descended on the herd. They worked the cows for a while before returning to camp.

"Well, we've had a successful hunt, Chief White Cloud," Paul said to Danny.

"Yes, Lone Wolf, I am very glad."

Paul took his watch out and bit his lip. "Oh my, it's after four. I need to head home right away." He jumped on Patsy and waved goodbye to his friends. "Thanks for the candy bars," he yelled as he left.

As he jolted along on Patsy's back, his tummy felt good, but his heart felt guilty.

Paul glanced into the window of Joe's shop as he passed. Joe saw him and waved. Paul felt even guiltier. His conscience kept bothering him. *Those candy bars were stolen, Paul. You had no right to eat them.*

Paul gave Patsy a kick. He was annoyed and wanted to cross the road quickly. Patsy gathered all the energy her chubby body could muster and trotted to the pasture. With no guidance, she passed through the gate and entered the field of sweet, fragrant clover. As Paul slipped off her back, she whinnied with delight and fell to grazing.

While Patsy was thoroughly enjoying herself, Paul was thoroughly miserable. He kicked at the stones in his path, dug his hands deep into his pockets, and started running for the big maple tree. The maple tree was Paul's place of solitude. Whenever he wanted to be alone, he climbed into its protection and mulled over his feelings. Sometimes his guilt drove him there, but at least his emotions stayed hidden under the leaves, and nobody asked any questions while Paul was in the tree.

Settling on a branch, Paul leaned against the trunk of the tree with his legs dangling in the breeze. Sunspots jumped up and down across his denim pants. Paul leaned over and looked at the ground way down below. *What if I fell down and died?* he thought. *I don't want to meet Jesus like this.*

Wayne interrupted Paul's thoughts by running across the yard. He stopped and peered up into the maple tree. "Come play with me," he said, motioning Paul to come down.

"Nah," Paul replied.

"Come on, let's go shoot some mice in the hay mow, or play in the pasture."

"I said I don't want to," Paul replied. "I'm busy digesting candy bars."

"You're what?" Wayne's ears perked up.

"Busy digesting candy bars that Danny gave to me," Paul repeated, grabbing a leaf and ripping it apart.

"Candy bars? Where did he get them? Did he get one for me?" Wayne asked hopefully.

"Nope, we ate them all." Paul grinned down at his little brother.

"I bet you stole them," Wayne declared, putting his hands on his hips and glaring up at Paul.

"I told you Danny gave them to me. That isn't stealing. And besides, it's none of your business."

Wayne ran off toward the house, bounded up the porch steps, and slammed the screen door behind him. Paul was relieved to see him go.

"Mom!" Wayne yelled.

"Yes?" Mom stepped out of the pantry to see what was wrong.

"Paul said he ate a bunch of candy bars."

"He did?"

"Yes, and he didn't even save one for me," Wayne pouted.

"Hmm, where did he get them?" Mom questioned.

"Well, he said Danny gave them to him, but I think he stole them," Wayne replied.

"We'll see," Mom said. "Run along and play. I'll have Dad talk to him about it."

A while later the screen door slammed. Peering through the leaves, Paul saw Dad coming toward the tree. "Paul?" Dad called sternly.

"Yes?"

"Come down here. I want to talk to you."

Paul climbed down reluctantly.

Dad did most of the talking. "Wayne came in a while ago and said Danny gave you some candy. Is that true?"

"He sure did," Paul replied.

"And how did he get his candy bars?"

"He got them from his dad's shop."

"I see. Did he ask his daddy for permission?"

"Not that I know of," Paul said.

"Just what I figured," Dad said, half to himself. "So Danny stole them and you ate them? Sounds like a pretty good deal for you. But guess what?"

"What?" Paul questioned.

"That's just as bad as if you had taken them yourself."

Paul hung his head and nodded.

"We're going over there before supper and you'll need to pay for the candy bars, confess that you stole them, and tell Joe you're sorry." Dad's face was stern and his shoulders set.

"But, Dad," Paul said, kicking the grass.

"Don't say 'but.' Say, 'Yes, Dad!' "

"Yes, Dad," Paul murmured.

That is how father and son found themselves walking into Joe's workshop. "Howdy do?" Joe said as he put down a piece of leather and walked over to Raymond and Paul. "What can I do for you?"

"Well, my son has something to tell you," Dad announced, squeezing Paul's shoulder.

"Oh, really?" Joe said in surprise. He bent forward and waited to hear what Paul had to say.

"I . . . um . . . ah . . . we boys took some candy bars from your shop today, and I'm . . . I'm really sorry. I'd like to pay for the ones I ate," Paul said awkwardly. His neck felt hot as he reached into his pocket and retrieved fifty cents. He handed the money to Joe.

"Well, that's mighty kind of you, Paul, to come and apologize to me," Joe said as he took the money. "I forgive you! This is a good reminder to me about always making our wrongs right so we can rest easy."

Paul nodded.

"Thank you, Joe," Raymond said. "We'd best be going home. My wife had supper almost ready and said it won't be long."

"Sure, sure," Joe answered. "See you later."

Father and son entered the kitchen, ready to dig

into Mom's famous chicken and mashed potatoes. As the family enjoyed their meal, Paul spent some time thinking about those candy bars. *They weren't as good as I thought they'd be. Stealing just isn't right. Next time I've got a sweet tooth, I'll need to buy a candy bar instead of stealing it!* Paul sighed to himself as he handed his plate to Mom for a second helping.

Chapter 4
"Here I Go! Watch Me!"

"Pride goeth before destruction,
and a haughty spirit before a fall."
—Proverbs 16:18

Paul shivered as his feet touched the cold hardwood floor. Quickly he grabbed his school clothes off the hook and hurried downstairs. As he opened the stairway door, he was met with a wave of warm air. It felt so good compared to the cold upstairs. Paul hurried over to the kitchen stove.

"Good morning, Paul!" Mom said, glancing Paul's way as she banged the last lunch box shut.

"Morning," Paul replied, pulling on his shirt and buttoning it up.

"You're always the last one up," Esther said as she took a drink of milk.

"Last one up, but the first one ready to go," Paul replied, his eyes twinkling.

Just then Paul looked outside and saw piles of snow everywhere. "Look outside, Esther!"

"I know," she replied, "there's more snow out there than we've had all winter."

"We probably won't even have school," Paul exclaimed.

"No, Paul, don't get such a notion in your head," Mom declared. "The snow plow cleared a path this morning, and Dad said that's all you'll need to get to school."

Paul sat on the wood box and pulled on his wool socks. Next he laced his black high-top shoes. "Now I'm ready for breakfast," he announced.

"Before you eat, Paul," Mom said, "I want you to braid Esther's hair for me."

"Aw, Mom, I don't want Paul to fix my hair," Esther protested.

"Esther!" Mom spoke sternly. "Baby John has been fussy all morning, and I've got so much work to do. Paul, come on, quickly now, obey—both of you."

Paul slowly inched his way over and positioned himself behind Esther. Esther turned and said with pleading eyes, "Please be gentle!"

"Oh, Esther," Paul grinned mischievously, "I'm getting so good at this that you shouldn't feel anything too severe."

Esther wasn't convinced, because just then Paul grabbed a fistful of hair and gave it a slight yank. "Ouch, not so rough!" Esther exclaimed, turning her head and glaring at Paul out of the corner of her eye.

Paul grinned some more. "Well, if you wouldn't move, it wouldn't hurt."

"Ach, Paul, now mind. Be gentle," Mom said as she rocked John and gently patted his back. John kept fussing and so did Esther. Lizzie Ann thought how much easier her life would be without all the fussing, but oh, it was all worth it. She loved her family!

Paul braided Esther's hair. His fingers felt rather clumsy as he tightened the rubber band securely at the end of each braid. Then he grabbed the braids and tickled Esther's ears with the ends. "Stop that!" Esther pouted as she grabbed a pigtail in each hand and jumped up from her perch.

Paul laughed and sat at the table to help himself to oatmeal and a glass of milk. After Paul had scraped his bowl clean, Dad called everyone into the living room for family devotions. Starting the day with God in mind was very important to Dad. After reading a chapter in Matthew, the whole family knelt down and asked God's blessing on the new day.

Devotions over, Paul jumped up and ran to the washbasin. He splashed cold water over his face. Then he slipped into his rubber boots, grabbed his thick winter coat and cap, and shouted, "See you later, Mom!"

"See you. Now be careful!" she called back.

"We will!" Paul answered. He and Wayne jumped down the porch steps and ran through the snow, laughing and whooping as they went.

The morning was enchanting. The evergreens along the road drooped under the snow. A cardinal hopped onto one of the snowy branches, sending a shower of snow to the ground below. The red bird puffed out his chest, lifted his head high, and called, "Cheer, cheer, whit, whit, whit, cheer!"

Paul watched the cardinal as he waited on Danny, Alvin, and the rest of the Bowman bunch. A few minutes later he heard someone puffing behind him. Turning, Paul saw Esther so bundled up in extra clothing that he wouldn't have recognized her had it not been for her eyes and the muffled shriek she gave as Wayne threw a snowball at her.

Finally the caravan of school-bound children was on its way. The boys frolicked in the snow, pushing and shoving each other. The girls walked more carefully, daintily picking up their skirts and lifting their boots high above the snow.

"You're a bunch of high steppers," Paul observed.

"We've got to be," said Esther. "We don't want to sit in school with snow dripping off our skirts." She glared at Paul as if he had no idea how to be careful and mannerly.

"I'm glad I'm a boy," Paul said, "and don't have to worry about such unnecessary things."

It seemed like a long time before the schoolhouse came into view. Paul's toes were ready for some warmth, and Esther was complaining that her fingers felt numb. When the children got closer, they all broke into a run toward the little building that held warmth and shelter.

The mudroom already had puddles of water that marked the entrance of other snow-ridden scholars. After removing their coats and kicking off their boots, the children made a quick dash for the coal stove on the east side of the schoolroom. All the students gathered there to thaw their cold hands and feet.

School began as usual with someone choosing a song. This morning it was Cristy who called out, "Song number nineteen." Everyone sang in unison, "When pangs of death seized on my soul, unto the

Lord I cried . . ."

Teacher Effie then led in prayer. Esther peeped over at Wayne, who had his eyes half open. As he glanced around, Esther caught his eye. She shook her head and shut her eyes. Promptly Wayne closed his curious eyes too.

"Third grade reading," Teacher Effie called. The third row of children stood up, grabbed their textbooks, and made their way to the long, narrow bench at the front of the room.

Several hours later Teacher Effie rang the bell for lunch break. Everyone scrambled to the shelves at the back of the room where they kept their lunch boxes and brought them back to their desks. After a satisfying lunch, the students hurried outside for a game of Fox and Geese. Paul loved the game and was disappointed when the bell rang.

When school was dismissed for the day, the children headed home. More snow had fallen and the drifts were much bigger. Some were so big they almost blocked the road.

The boys started trying to see who could jump into the deepest drift. "Look at me," Wayne yelled, standing in snow up to his chest.

"Watch this!" Danny shouted as he jumped off the bank and into the ditch.

"That's just like boys!" exclaimed Esther, shivering. "Imagine all the snow in their boots."

"Yeah," said Ella, "and once they start they don't know when to quit!" The girls walked primly on, hand in hand, as the boys bounded from one drift to another.

When they reached the top of the last hill, Paul took a run for the bank on which his family's windmill stood. When Paul reached the top of the steep bank, he called out, "Here I go! Watch me!"

Then he leaped into the air. When he hit the snow, he kept sinking deeper and deeper and deeper.

Esther gasped. "Oh, no!"

They couldn't see him anymore. Paul had disappeared into the snow.

When Wayne realized that Paul was in trouble, he dashed toward the house as fast as his legs could carry him. Flinging open the door, he cried, "Dad! Dad! Come quick! Hurry! Paul's dying!"

While Wayne was going to get help, Paul was trying hard to get out of the snowdrift. He pounded the snow around him with his fists and stomped with all his might. Snow was everywhere: around him, on top of him, and beneath him. The harder he tried to get free, the more frantic he became. He stomped some more, his breathing coming in rapid gasps. The oxygen in his little cave was diminishing rapidly. He felt faint and dizzy.

In the meantime, Mom came out of the living room with worry written all over her face. "Where . . . what . . . who . . . what did you say?" But there was no answer. She looked out the window just in time to see Dad and Wayne running down the lane and onto the road. Dad carried a broom in one hand and was trying to get his other hand into the armhole of his insulated vest.

Paul inched up higher as he packed the snow underneath his feet, but he knew he wasn't mounting

41

fast enough. He needed oxygen right away! *I'm going to die if somebody doesn't help me*, he thought. Just when he felt like slumping in a heap under the snow, he thought he heard his dad's deep voice. Had Dad come to rescue him?

When Dad got to the snowdrift, Esther quickly told him exactly where Paul went down. "There, see that hole? He went down until we couldn't see him anymore."

Dad furiously flailed his broom back and forth close to where a little dent could be seen in the snow. Snow flew everywhere as he tried to reach his son. Finally he reached down and grabbed at a dark spot in the snow. It was a denim coat. He lifted it higher and higher, grunting as he pulled Paul up on the bank. Paul reached up to wipe his snow-covered face and then lay gasping. Pure air had never felt so good to his hungry lungs. He looked up into the loving eyes of his daddy and whispered, "Thank you." Tears threatened to fall as he looked into Dad's eyes.

Paul started shivering uncontrollably. He was too weak to walk, so Dad lifted him in his arms and carried him. A subdued group of children followed Dad home. Esther picked up the broom and Paul's lunch box. She shivered, thinking about the accident. *Now I know why Mom always says to be careful!*

Mom was standing at the window, anxiously watching for her husband and son. She could see Paul was alive. Relieved, she breathed a prayer, "Thank you, Lord!" Then she hurried to the closet and grabbed a warm blanket. When Dad and Paul entered the house, Mom was ready for them and wrapped her cold boy in the blanket. Then she scurried around the kitchen, working quickly all the while. Pots clanged as she heated up water for tea and filled a basin with water for Paul's icy feet.

Dad got a little twinkle in his eye as he watched his wife scurry around. It seemed her apron strings floated along behind her. It was a good wife he had married, and she worked very hard. *Why, even I have a hard time keeping up with her busy hands,* he thought as he helped her carry the basin of water.

He turned to Paul. "Well, son, I want to hear the whole story when you're feeling a little better." Raymond squeezed his son's shoulder and headed out to the broiler house to start the evening chores.

At the supper table, Paul told his family the whole story—how they were jumping into the drifts all the way home from school and how it felt beneath the snow. Esther interrupted his story to say, "Yes, but if you wouldn't have been showing off, it wouldn't have happened."

Dad cocked his head and looked at Paul. "Is that true?"

Paul wriggled in his seat and nodded sheepishly.

"Well," said Dad, "may this be a lesson to all of us never to show off! If Paul would have been under that snow only a few minutes longer, he could have died from showing off." He looked over at Paul. "Paul, don't forget the Bible says in Proverbs 16:18, "Pride goeth before destruction, and a haughty spirit before a fall.""

Paul never forgot.

43

Chapter 5
All for a Lollipop

"Let him that stole steal no more."
—Ephesians 4:28

One cold Saturday Paul and his dad headed for the town of Mt. Hope. Dad had to stop at the hardware store to exchange some bolts. Then he planned to visit a friend and fellow minister to talk about some issues they faced in the church. Mom and Dad decided that Paul would stay at his cousin Al's house until Dad was ready to go home. Paul was thrilled with the idea. Al and Paul always had so much fun together. They hunted sparrows, dammed the creek, dug burrows in the haymow, made snow forts, and did whatever else they could together. The two boys were inseparable friends.

It was early afternoon when Dad and Paul got to Al's house. Grey clouds were gathering in the west, and the wind was starting to whistle through the pine trees. Al was delighted to have Paul at his house. "Do you want to see my new rabbits?" Al asked.

"Sure!" Paul replied, and with that the boys raced to the barn.

For a few hours, the boys played in the barn.

They held the rabbits for a while. Then they started making tunnels in the hay. In one corner they stacked up hay bales to make a fort. Eventually they tired of playing in the hay and meandered around the barn in search of mice. When at last it was too dark to see, the boys sat down on some feed sacks to discuss what they should do next.

"We might as well get my chores done," Al decided, grabbing a bucket and filling it with feed for the chickens.

"That's fine with me," Paul replied, picking up another bucket. When the two boys had all the animals satisfied, they walked to the house, snow crunching beneath their feet.

"My, I'm really hungry!" Al said.

"Me too!" Paul replied. "And I'm not worried, because your mom always has something good to eat, just like my mom!" Lydia Ann, Al's mother, was a twin sister to Paul's mom, Lizzie Ann. In Paul's mind, Lydia Ann's cooking was just as fine as his mother's. Sure enough, when the boys stepped in the door, their noses confirmed that a good supper awaited them.

After supper, Paul and Al needed to go to the schoolhouse to fix the fire. This was another of Al's daily chores during the winter.

Paul shivered as he walked. The cold wind nipped at his nose and forced its way through the sturdy denim that covered his legs. "Sure is cold tonight," Al commented.

"At least we don't have to walk a mile to get to school!" Paul exclaimed.

"Yes, don't you wish you lived this close?" Al asked.

"It would be nice!" Paul admitted. "But we've had a lot of fun walking home from school, you know."

"Yes, I suppose," Al replied, retrieving the key from his pocket and handing it to Paul. "You go unlock the school door and I'll grab some coal from the coal shed."

As Paul opened the door, its rusty hinges let out a low squeak. He crossed the room and opened the stove door. The flames had died down, and it was time for some more coal. Al came in carrying two buckets of coal. Together the boys poured the heavy buckets into the stove. They left the door open until the flames started to lick at the new coal.

"I just thought of a good idea," Paul said with a twinkle in his eye.

"What's that?" Al replied.

"Wouldn't a lollipop hit the spot right now?"

"It sure would. I'd say we deserve it for doing the chores," Al answered. "In fact, for all the times I've trudged over here, not once have I gotten a single cent."

Both boys knew exactly where the lollipops were stowed: in the bottom right-hand drawer of Teacher Effie's desk. Underneath the answer key books was a bag of lollipops. They were no ordinary lollipops either. They were BIG! Each one was swirled with bright colors, all in different flavors. Al and Paul knew this because Al had received one for winning a spelling bee and had gladly shared it with Paul.

They stopped in front of Teacher Effie's desk, contemplating. Outside, the sun was slowly setting,

making the schoolroom dusky and dim. There was a rustle of papers as Paul and Al reached under the answer key books and each retrieved a lollipop from the drawer. They ripped off the wrappers and threw them into the stove. The heat from the coal fire warmed them as they licked the wonderful-tasting lollipops. "Mmm," Al murmured in satisfaction, "I love this kind!"

"Me too!" Paul exclaimed. "Teacher Effie will never find out we took two. She's got so many in that pack, she won't miss them, and besides, we deserve it!"

"I know," Al said, his tongue busy licking his lollipop.

The lollipop thieves stayed in the schoolhouse until they were sure they would have the lollipops finished by the time they reached home. Then they locked the door and slowly meandered back to Al's house through the gathering darkness. Those lollipops were delicious! The wonderful taste overrode the thought of sin for the time being.

By the time they reached the sidewalk in front of Al's house, the lollipops were gone and everything appeared normal. At the hitching post stood faithful Betty. "Well, looks like Dad's here and ready to go," Paul said as the door opened and Dad bid Al's family goodbye.

"Ready, son?" Dad called.

"I guess so," Paul said as he slowly turned and ambled toward the buggy.

"See you tomorrow, Al," Paul called, waving as he climbed up into the buggy.

"See you!" Al said. He grabbed a handful of snow and started licking it as Dad and Paul started out the lane.

Betty knew her way home without any guidance, and she knew she didn't have far to go to get there. The promise of hay, oats, and water called to her hungry stomach as she ran the whole way. Paul loved it when Betty acted like this. It seemed as if they were flying.

The next day Paul went to church with his family, and not once did he think about the stolen lollipops.

XXXXX

On Monday morning the school bell rang as normal, and everyone ran to their desks and sat down. Teacher Effie called out the usual greeting, "Good morning, children."

The students replied, "Good morning, Teacher." They sang a few songs and prayed a prayer of blessing on another school day.

This particular morning, though, they didn't start classes as usual. Teacher Effie cleared her throat and said, "Before classes begin, I've got something I need to know." She glanced around the room and continued, "This morning I was looking through my desk and found two lollipops missing from my drawer." She shook her index finger. "I want those who stole them to confess by tomorrow morning or there will be a punishment for all of you." Teacher Effie's voice was stern and the color rose in her cheeks as she gazed at her students' faces.

Even the innocent ones quailed at her look. But there were two boys who shuddered a little more and felt a great deal hotter than any of the rest.

In the heavy silence, Effie mused. *I wish they would all come to attention like this when classes are called.* Her heart smiled at the thought of having a classroom this reverent. It was only a few years ago that Effie had made a resolution as to what form of discipline she would use in the classroom: *I'll discipline in love as the Lord helps me.* Teaching had many rewards, but boys who tried and tested her resolve to discipline with love were still a grief to Effie.

Effie stopped her musing and called the first class of the day.

After school that day, two boys headed for the coal shed instead of toward home. They had some important matters to discuss. "What are we going to do?" Al wondered, looking at Paul for an answer.

"I don't know," Paul replied. "I don't want to confess."

"Me neither," Al said, staring at the pile of coal at his feet, "but I don't want a punishment either."

"No, I don't want a punishment," Paul said, biting his lip. "Maybe we should just go in and confess to the teacher now, rather than in front of everybody tomorrow morning."

"Yeah, but what if we just skip it all? What do you think would happen?" Al asked.

"Probably the same thing that happened last time nobody confessed. Everybody got punished, and that isn't right either," Paul replied.

"I guess you're right." Al kicked a piece of coal across the floor. "We might as well get it over with."

Slowly the two boys left the shed and went around the schoolhouse to the basement door. The hinges creaked, giving them more jitters than they already had. Both boys felt hot, ashamed, and nervous. "Yes, boys, what can I do for you?" Teacher Effie said quietly when the boys suddenly entered her classroom. She had an idea what was wrong with her two students.

Paul spoke first, "Um, well, we came to say we're sorry. We ate those two lollipops."

"I see," Effie said slowly.

"Uh-huh, we're terribly sorry we did it," Al added, nervously shifting from one foot to the other.

Teacher Effie got up from her chair. Circling around her desk, she put her hands on the boys' shoulders and said, "I'm so glad you two were men enough to say you were wrong. I don't want it to happen again and I'll forgive you for it." She smiled and added, "Go on home now, boys. You're forgiven."

Two lighthearted boys bounded out the door, calling back, "See you, Teacher!" Outside they stopped, sighing with relief. Paul said, "Al, I don't ever want to steal again. I'm going to pray that God will help me."

"Me too!" Al said as he waved goodbye.

In the schoolhouse, Teacher Effie was deep in thought. *If I'm reading them right, those two boys were mighty sorrowful a few minutes ago. It's amazing how confessing sin makes one feel so much better inside. There is nothing like having peace with God and others, and in your own heart.* When the last book was put away and the last test had been scored, Teacher Effie left the schoolhouse and headed toward home. She felt lighter in her own heart because two boys had confessed their sin. Philippians 4:7 kept coming to her mind. "And the peace of God, which passeth all understanding, shall keep your hearts and minds through Christ Jesus."

Part Two:
Finding God

Chapter 6
A Cloud of Terror

*"There is no fear in love; but perfect love casteth
out fear: because fear hath torment. He that feareth
is not made perfect in love."*
—1 John 4:18

A shaking boy lay under the warm quilt. He wasn't shaking because he was cold. It was the middle of summer, and although the sun had set behind the distant hills a long time ago, it was still a warm seventy-five degrees in the house. The shaking continued from Paul's bed. Was he sick? Perhaps crying? It really was strange to be covered so warmly on such a night. Not the slightest of breezes entered the open window in his bedroom. No sound could be heard from under the covers, but Paul was wide awake and shaking from head to toe. Even though it would be morning in only a few hours, Paul hadn't slept a wink yet that night.

He was scared, so dreadfully scared that he had tugged the covers up over his already warm head. Sweat soaked his quilt. Every night for the last month he'd had trouble going to sleep, but not because he wasn't tired. No, the reason Paul could not sleep was because he was terrified. He was bombarded with thoughts like, *You're a sinner,*

Paul. Tomorrow might be the day you die, and if you do, you'll go straight to hell. On and on the accusations went. Paul's soft bed did little to make him comfortable against his guilty conscience. *Paul, what if Jesus comes tonight?*

Paul's mind was running wild. *Do I hear someone coming up the steps? No, probably just the house creaking.* An owl hooted outside his window, and Paul jumped. *What if tonight Jesus opens the sky like a scroll? I know I'm not ready to meet Jesus.* His conscience kept speaking to him for hours on end.

Amid all these questions, Paul would hear another voice, quite different from the first. The one who created lies, the devil, was filling Paul's mind with false assurance. "Oh, Paul, you aren't that bad. Why, if Jesus would come tonight, He would let you into heaven. After all, how bad can a twelve-year-old boy be? Just go to sleep. Everything is okay."

Paul was caught in the middle of a great battle between good and evil. The voice of the Holy Spirit, sent from God, was prompting him to exchange his evil heart for one that was pure and good. This night, just like all the nights before, Paul chose to believe the devil's lies once again. As the moon sank below the horizon, Paul finally settled into a restless sleep.

xxxxx

It had started last winter with fears about everything. One evening, while climbing down the chicken house stairs to fix the fire in the coal boiler, Paul thought a man was coming to get him. He could almost feel a hand squeezing his throat. Paul shoveled coal into the boiler as fast as he could. A spider web swept across his face, and silly as it may seem, Paul was terrified. He grabbed a broom leaning against the wall and jabbed the end into every dark corner. He was going to catch that man before the man caught him. But in reality, Paul was already caught—caught in a web of fear. He was tightly bound and didn't know how to escape. He wanted freedom. He needed help, but how could he get it?

The imaginary man who wanted to catch him was not the only thing Paul feared. He hated the thought of going down the creaky stairs to the fruit cellar to fetch fruit for Mom. Any darkness was a horrible enemy. Paul was also afraid of the neighbor man who was mentally handicapped. When Paul saw the man, Paul ran with all his might just to distance himself from the man, afraid of what would happen if he got close.

Paul didn't want to die. He was so terribly afraid.

xxxxx

Another night came and with it came another looming cloud of fear. Paul lay under the quilt, wet with sweat. If the Lord returned that night, Paul was convinced the Lord wouldn't find him under the quilt. Paul was so sure of this that he stayed under that quilt for most of those hot summer nights. Paul was afraid of what God would do if He found him. He didn't want the gates of heaven locked against him, but neither was he willing to give Jesus his heart so he could enter through those gates. For weeks, Paul trembled in fear of death.

Autumn came, and one evening Dad opened the screen door and excitedly called in from the porch, "Children, come quickly! I want to show you something." The whole family assembled on the front lawn and gazed at the sky as it flashed blue and red. Truly, it was an awesome sight! For Paul, though, it was terribly frightening. *Is Jesus coming back? Oh, I'm not ready to meet Him. What is going on?*

The lights in the sky were the northern lights, not the second coming of the Lord. But Paul's fear gripped his heart that evening; he couldn't forget how he felt. Paul knew he wasn't prepared for heaven. Often he wondered, *How can I get rid of this fear? Should I ask Dad to help me? Surely there is a way to get rid of this.*

Dad had always said, "Only through Jesus are we able to live without fear." Paul wondered just what Dad meant by those words. Paul believed Dad knew what he was saying. He was Paul's hero. Dad seemed to know everything.

Over and over the same questions crept into Paul's mind and gripped his heart. *How can I find peace? Can God help me? What if the end of the world would come?* Paul did not pray or read his Bible very much, so he did not find verses in the New Testament on overcoming fear. Only God could save Paul from this dark, looming cloud of fear.

Chapter 7
Forgiveness in
the Feed Room

"If we confess our sins, he is faithful and just to forgive us our sins, and to cleanse us from all unrighteousness."
—1 John 1:9

It was just another long, miserable March day for Paul. All through the day a voice kept telling him, "Paul, give your heart to me and I'll make you a new person."

Then another voice would whisper, "There's nothing wrong. You're a good boy. Just forget all you have done wrong and it will be okay." But nothing was okay. Not only was Paul miserable and frightened, but he was also sick and tired of the questions that haunted him all day and all night. The howling winter winds only added to Paul's misery.

The clanging of spoons and forks could be heard three times a day in the big white farmhouse. This time it was at the supper table, and Mom had made chicken, mashed potatoes, and corn. Nothing tasted quite as good as Mom's cooking (that's what Dad always said). Paul's mouth was stuffed, but the taste wasn't as good as usual. Mom peered at Paul and shook her head. Paul knew she had seen him take a huge mouthful. "Ach, Paul, eat a little slower and don't shovel it in so." But Mom didn't know the turmoil in Paul's troubled heart.

Paul's mouth was dry. He gulped down some water, ate another bite, and washed the food down with another swallow of water. At last the agonizing meal was over. Before anyone could leave the table, Dad wanted to know who was going to help him shovel coal into the chicken house boiler. Ever since Dad's back injury, the boys had been taking turns helping him. Tonight was Wayne's turn, but Paul said, "I'll do it for you, Wayne."

Wayne's whooping and hollering was silenced by Mom. "Wayne, do be more quiet. John just went to sleep and here you are hollering so loud."

"Okay, Mom. I was just so glad Paul is taking my turn. Come on, Mary, let's go finish the puzzle." The two ran to their spots around the jigsaw puzzle.

As Paul walked to the chicken house with Dad, he kicked at the frozen ground. *How am I going to tell Dad? Will he understand what's the matter with me? I've got to talk to him. I need to tell him how I feel.* Paul opened the door to the feed room. Together the two silently descended into the basement. As Dad opened the furnace door, Paul noticed the red-hot coal bed. He grabbed a shovel and started shoveling coal into the furnace. The hot flames licked at the fresh coal, rising higher. The heat became more intense. *Oh! It must be awful to die and end up in the everlasting flames. Should I tell Dad about my struggles?*

After the furnace was filled, Paul put the shovel away and went up the dusty stairway into the dimly lit feed room. Dad set the gas lantern down for a bit while he checked the feed.

"Uh, Dad . . . um, I want to talk to you," Paul stammered. Dad turned and gave his full attention to his son. Paul continued. "Well, it's like this. I just don't feel right. I'm afraid Jesus will come back and I'm not ready and I'm . . . I'm afraid to die, Dad." Paul gulped and bit his lip as tears coursed down his cheeks. "What can I do?"

There was a moment's pause as Dad looked down at Paul. Gently, Dad said, "You need Jesus inside your heart. That's what you need!" Dad nodded his head in agreement to his own words. "It will give you peace and take away your fear of dying. First John 1:9 says, 'If we confess our sins, he is faithful and just to forgive us our sins, and to cleanse us from all unrighteousness.'"

Paul nodded and wiped at his tears.

Dad's arm reached around his boy's shoulders as he spoke. "Paul, do you know you're a sinner?"

Paul nodded again.

"Do you want to ask Jesus to come inside your heart and take your sins away and make you born again?"

Again Paul nodded. By now, the tears were flowing in steady streams.

"Paul, do you believe that God can take away your sins?"

Yet again Paul nodded.

"Well," Dad said, "let's kneel down here and you tell God all the wrong things you've done. Then ask Him to forgive you and to come into your heart.

After you're done, I'll pray."

Paul's prayer was filled with tears and sobs as he began to tell Jesus, the One who can save from sin, all the sins he remembered committing. Dad's hand on his shoulder gave him the courage to pray. "Dear Jesus, I've been such a bad person. I'm a horrible sinner. Jesus, I want you to forgive me . . . please give me a new heart."

Then Dad prayed, "Help him, dear Lord, that he would never turn his back toward you again. Thank you, Father, for Paul's desire to do what is right. Keep him now under your wings and may he be kept from the devil's snares. Amen."

Paul looked up at Dad and noticed tears in his eyes. At his look, Dad said, "Paul, it's not because I'm sad; it's just that I'm so glad. Do you feel at peace now?"

"Yes, I do," Paul's head nodded emphatically. "I've never felt like this before. I have peace with God!"

In the dim light of the gas lantern, father and son hugged each other. There was happiness on Paul's face that had never been there before.

"Paul, I want you to read your Bible every day now. As soon as we get into the house, I want you to read 1 John 2 and Romans 8."

"Yes, I want to start reading the Bible!" Paul's eyes shone in anticipation.

Dad and Paul walked toward the house, both of them too deep in thought to notice the noises of the evening.

After evening prayers that night, Dad joined Paul in his room. Dad showed him where to find the book of 1 John and told him to start reading there. After Dad left him, Paul eagerly devoured the words of the first two chapters, continuing on to the third, and all the way to chapter five.

A knock sounded on the door. It was Dad. "Paul, I know you love reading the Bible, but it's eleven o'clock and you really need to get to bed." Paul didn't want to go to bed, but for a different reason than before. His bed had been a place of misery and fear for months, but now it was different. Now he didn't want to go to bed because he wanted to keep reading the Bible.

"Oh, it's so wonderful to read the Bible, Dad! I could go on all night!"

"Yes, I know, son, but tomorrow you have work to do, and if you're up all night, you won't be worth a lot tomorrow."

Paul closed the Bible. Oh, the words in it made so much more sense, and Paul loved the Word as he never had before. He blew out the lamp and talked to God until his breathing became deep and restful.

He hadn't slept so well since . . . Paul could hardly remember!

Paul's life was dramatically changed after his new birth. Not only did Dad and Mom see the great change that had taken place in Paul's heart, but his friends also noticed. The sins he once loved were now hated. His rebellion was gone. He was a new creature, just like the Bible says in 2 Corinthians 5:17, "Therefore if any man be in Christ, he is a new creature: old things are passed away; behold, all things are become new."

Chapter 8
A New Believer

"For if our heart condemn us, God is greater than our heart, and knoweth all things."
—1 John 3:20

Paul was a free boy since he had found God and become born again. He felt so good inside! His waking hours were filled with song, and his evening Bible reading refreshed his soul. Paul was hungry for God. Many a dark night he walked outside to a little spot behind the chicken house where he would talk to God. Paul would pray out loud and feel so close to his heavenly Father!

Paul was very happy. That is, until one morning when he awoke and something felt drastically wrong. He felt as though he had committed some awful sin. Paul didn't feel a bit of God's presence. What had happened? Throughout the entire day, whether in the barn, in the pasture, or at the table, he thought and thought of all he had done in the last few days. Paul just could not think of any sin he had committed. Oh, it was such an awful feeling. It felt like his old life again. He fell on his knees and cried out, "God, what did I do? Where are you?" But everything was silent. Paul cried, "God, have you left me?" He even asked God to forgive him for the sins he had confessed when he became a Christian, but he still could not feel the peace he had when he first became born again.

A few nights later Paul was on his knees out beside the old chicken house again, praying. "Why aren't you there, God? Where are you? Don't you hear me? Please forgive all my sins. I want you in my life."

Over the next several days, Paul continued to plead with God to forgive every sin he could remember ever committing. He was struggling under a heavy feeling of guilt—he didn't even feel like a Christian. Prayer times felt dull and meaningless. Evening Bible readings were dry too. The bridge of communication between God and him seemed broken, but why? What had he done? He felt so guilty, but as far as he knew, he wasn't trying to hide anything in his life. Paul had confessed all his wrongs when he had knelt down and prayed beside Dad in the feed room.

One morning as the sun peeked over the far eastern hills and cast its beams to the west, Paul awoke, yawned, and stretched. A fresh new day had dawned. He felt so good this morning he wanted to sing. Why, he felt like a Christian again! The peace was back in Paul's heart. He couldn't explain why, but he felt God was very near. Just yesterday he had felt as though God was not with him, but now God's nearness seemed so real. What had happened? No guilt, no anxiety, and no bad feelings were left. It was all gone. Paul was free again. All day long he felt free and, oh, God seemed so close again.

The freedom lasted a week. Then the terrible feeling of guilt came over Paul again, like a storm cloud lashing its fury on his heart. Paul wondered whether he'd ever feel close to God again.

One evening while looking for something to read, a little book caught Paul's eye. The book was titled *How To Get Assurance*, written by B. Charles Hostetler. One story in particular changed Paul's life.

Mr. Hostetler was getting married. He was excited at the prospect of spending the rest of his life being the husband of this lovely young lady. At the ceremony, Charles and his bride stepped up to the podium and vowed to love and cherish each other "until death do us part." As the minister pronounced them man and wife, Charles thought, *I don't feel like a husband.* He didn't feel like a husband the entire day. Did that change his position as a husband? No, it didn't matter whether he felt like a husband or not. He was still married. He accepted the fact that he was married regardless of his feelings. He just believed it. Years went by, and Charles and his wife had a wonderful life together.

The truth revealed in this story struck deep into Paul's heart. He had been a believer in Christ for only a few months, and many times he didn't feel like a Christian, just like the newlywed husband who didn't feel married immediately after the wedding ceremony. Paul decided to believe that he was a Christian, even when he didn't feel like one.

After reading the booklet, Paul felt much better. He had been basing his life on feelings instead of on faith. Now he knew he was forgiven because he had confessed and repented of his past sins. Paul hadn't understood that peace was a position, not merely a feeling. Sometimes his position brought him good feelings and sometimes it didn't bring him any special feelings at all, but now he knew that his feelings didn't change his position. Paul was learning that it took faith to believe God forgave him and freed him from his sins even when his feelings said just the opposite. He claimed 1 John 1:9. "If we confess our sins, he is faithful and just to forgive us our sins, and to cleanse us from all unrighteousness."

The most important thing Paul learned through these experiences was that the person who is born again lives by faith, not by feelings. He liked the verse in Hebrews 10:38 that says, "The just shall live by faith." It showed him that his thoughts may not be based on his feelings, but rather on faith and truth. First John 3:20 also helped him understand this truth. In this verse, the Greek word for "heart" includes the connotation of "feelings." By exchanging the word "heart" for the word "feelings," the verse reads like this: "For if our [feelings] condemn us, God is greater than our [feelings], and knoweth all things."

Chapter 9
A Burden to Tell

*"Go . . . to thy friends, and tell them how
great things the Lord hath done for thee."*
—Mark 5:19

I t was a beautiful day for groundhog hunting.
Paul grabbed his gun and bullets. After a bit
of hesitation, he stuffed a little booklet titled
Christian Workers Handbook into his pocket as well.

Paul had invited Al to go hunting with him.
Al readily agreed, so at five o'clock they met at
Grandpa's creek bottom, which was about halfway
between their houses. They liked to go to Grandpa's
creek bottom in the spring to watch him tap maple
trees for sap and boil it into syrup, but it was also a
good meeting place throughout the year whenever
the teenaged boys went on adventures together.

On his way to the creek, Paul prayed, "Jesus,
open the doors so I can tell Al about what you can
do. You know he has started following the wrong
crowd. Help me say the right things. Give me a
chance to talk about you. Help him become born
again. Amen."

A low whistle sounded. Paul looked up as he
swung his leg over the barbed wire fence. Al sat

beside a tree, his beagle pup, Mindy, at his side.

"Hey, Paul, I sure hope we get to see some groundhogs today! Mindy seems to think she's in for some excitement. She's been tugging at the leash ever since I grabbed my gun." Al picked up his single-shot rifle and added, "I thought we should check the east fields first and then come around to the west. That would give us a little time to see if anything comes out of that hole I walked past on my way over here." Al was intent on getting at least one of the groundhogs that were such a pest to farmers.

"Sounds good to me," Paul replied, and with that the two boys walked into the field. They studied the ground, carefully checking for hidden holes and beaten paths. They stealthily crept along the fencerow as Mindy sniffed and pulled at the leash. As the boys approached an unusually large groundhog hole, they noticed a big granddaddy groundhog munching on some grass close to his second hole, fifty yards away. Oblivious to the two hunters, the groundhog continued eating.

With careful aim, Al pulled the trigger. *Pow!*

"I think you got him, Al," Paul exclaimed as Mindy let out a howl. They moved in closer and saw that the groundhog really was dead. "He won't be digging another hole in our field for the horses to step in and break their legs. No sir," Paul said, grinning at Al, who was checking to see how good a shot he had made.

Paul and Al continued walking through the fields, hoping for another shot, but they didn't see any more groundhogs. They entered the last field and decided it was time for a rest. The two boys sat on the bank beside the bubbling creek. They started chatting, and it was then Paul could tell God was answering his prayers about speaking to Al. "You know, Al, it's so important to be ready to meet Jesus because He might come tonight." Paul spoke with such seriousness that Al turned and looked at him. Al's eyebrows furrowed as he thought about Jesus coming again.

Paul prayed silently for wisdom as he spoke to Al of his newfound faith. "I was so miserable with no peace, and oh, I was so afraid of dying! Then I asked Dad to help me, and he told me I needed to repent of my sins, confess them, and ask Jesus to come into my life to become born again. And that's what I did! I can't tell you how glad I've been ever since. It's been wonderful." Paul's eyes were moist as he told Al of all the wonderful things that God had done for him. "Oh, and do you remember how I told you I had such a terrible time sleeping at night, and how I'd get afraid over little things?"

"Yes, I remember you said something about it," Al replied.

"Well, I don't have a problem with being afraid anymore, and I've been sleeping the whole night through." Paul's eyes shone. "Just to be free from those struggles has been wonderful."

The sun had cast its last rays and darkness was filling the valley, but Paul wasn't thinking about the darkness around them. Paul had a burden for the darkness in Al's heart.

"Well, I guess I might as well tell you that I've really been struggling lately." Al bit his lip as he spoke. "I kept telling God I wasn't ready yet, and every time I said that, I felt awfully guilty. But lately I haven't felt convicted and that feeling of guilt has gone away. I've been wishing that feeling of guilt would come back again."

A tingle of immense joy spread through Paul's body as Al shared his feelings. God was answering his prayers. Paul then asked Al a question he had wanted to ask for weeks. "Al, would you want to become born again like I did?"

Al gazed into the gathering darkness and for a long time didn't say a word. Then he murmured, "Yes, I think I would. But how does a person become born again?"

"Well, I don't know what to tell you except to do exactly what I did. We've got to kneel down and pray, and when you pray, ask God to forgive you for all the bad things you've done. Tell God everything you did; then He will wash your sins away. Tell Him you're sorry and that from now on you want to follow and listen only to Him. Oh, and ask Him to help you live right so you can always be ready to die. That's what Dad told me to do, and I found peace," Paul replied.

Paul and Al knelt down in the soft grass on the creek bank. The water below them bubbled and gurgled lazily, but neither gave heed to the sound. The boys forgot about groundhogs as Al opened his heart to receive the Living Water. All heaven rejoiced as another soul was added to the kingdom of God.

As Al confessed his wrongs to Jesus, tears ran down his cheeks. When he finally opened his eyes after praying, Al felt like a different person. Peace like he'd never known, freedom from the guilt of sin, and hope for the future—everything he really wanted was there.

As they sat down on the bank again, Paul asked Al the same question Dad had asked him in the feed room. "Do you have peace, Al?"

"Oh, yes," Al said. "I feel so good! I know I have been forgiven."

The two boys walked home in the dusk, surrounded by the awesome power of God's presence. Their hearts were light and free.

The effects of Al's heart change did not end there alongside the rippling creek. They were displayed everywhere Al went. He was a different person than before. Al loved God and wanted to follow Him, and the wrong crowd he had been with permanently lost a member.

One of the first things God gave Al was a burden for his friends, the same kind of burden that Paul had. Al could not be silent about what God had done. A few months later Al's sister, Verna, made a commitment to follow God. She had seen the miraculous change in Al's life and wanted the same thing to happen in her own heart. Al's influence pointed Verna to God.

God was working the impossible. In an Amish community where hearts had turned toward sin, God was changing lives. Paul and Al became deeply burdened for others who were under the bondage of sin's temptations. The boys wanted, no, needed to tell others about salvation. They felt they especially needed to tell their school friends about what God had done in their lives. Many times they prayed together and talked about the shared longing to have their friends come to know God in a deep, personal way.

XXXXX

It was a cold and snowy winter evening when Paul and Al decided they needed talk to Aden, their friend from school, about Jesus. Paul hitched up Betty and drove the mile to pick up Al. Next they headed to Aden's big farmhouse at the end of a long lane.

Betty's muzzle was frosty by the time the buggy stopped at the hitching post at Aden's place. Betty shook her head from side to side, trying to get rid of the ice beads that hung around her mouth and nose. Paul gently warmed her muzzle with his gloved hands and Betty gave a soft whinny. She was a good family horse, but everything had to be just right for her. She didn't like ice hanging from her mouth.

As Al and Paul made their way to the door, the soft glow of a lantern in the window shone out onto the frozen lawn. The two boys were eager for a little warmth, and it looked like Aden's house was a good place to find it. Paul knocked on the door.

"Why, hello snowmen," came the friendly greeting from Ezra, Aden's dad. "I suppose you two came to chat with Aden. Come right on in. He's around here somewhere."

Aden came down from upstairs and smiled. "How do? It's not very often that I get company. Have a seat." The boys visited with Aden's parents for a while. Ezra wanted to know how everyone was in their families and whether they had done any trapping yet. In the meantime, Ezra's wife hurried around the kitchen in search of a bit of food to warm the boys' stomachs. She succeeded in finding a few molasses cookies and served them with fresh milk.

"We didn't expect any food, but this sure hits the spot," Paul said after the last crumbs disappeared.

Aden turned to Paul and Al. "Did you want to go up to my room to talk?" The boys nodded, and the three headed upstairs. They all found seats on Aden's bed.

Al opened the conversation. "I guess we should tell you why we came tonight. Lately Paul changed his life around and decided to follow Jesus, and so did I. We just felt we needed to come over tonight and tell you what Jesus did for us and see if you wanted the same." Al turned to Paul and said, "You tell him what happened to you."

Paul then shared how he used to be afraid, how he dreaded every night, and how his fear of dying made him try to hide under the quilt. He explained about the night he gave his heart to Jesus and was born again. "Jesus said in John 3, 'Ye must be born again,' " Paul explained. "I confessed all the sins I remembered committing, and God gave me a peace that is indescribable. Nights have been so peaceful, and I'm not afraid anymore. Jesus really changed me," Paul concluded.

Aden glanced at Paul and then looked away. Finally he said, "Well, I know I'm a sinner, but I know I'll have to get rid of some of my gods first before I can give my heart to Jesus." Aden pointed toward the radio that sat on his nightstand. "That thing, for instance, is my god."

"Oh, but Aden, you don't understand. You don't need to get rid of those things first. You need to come to God just the way you are, confess your sins, and ask Him to come in and change your life. He'll give you the power to make those changes after that," Paul replied as he paged through the little Testament he had pulled out of his pocket. He prayed silently that God would show him a verse for Aden.

"I know a verse that would explain that," Al exclaimed. "First John 1:9: 'If we confess our sins, he is faithful and just to forgive us our sins, and to cleanse us from all unrighteousness.' That means that if we confess, He'll forgive us, and after that He'll cleanse us. That makes sense, doesn't it?"

"Yes, that does make it plain, but I'm still not sure whether God will accept me the way I am now." Aden's doubts were real, yet his furrowed brow and worried expression as he sat on his bed made it obvious he was under conviction.

"Well, Aden, God won't accept you into heaven if you're living the way you are now. But if you pray to Him and give Him your life, and confess all those gods as sin, He will forgive you and accept you into His kingdom." Paul's heart was heavy as he looked at Aden. "Would you like to pray and pour out your heart to God?"

"Yes, I would," Aden nodded. The three boys knelt on the hardwood floor and Aden prayed. "God, I know I'm a sinner. Please forgive me for all my sins. I'm so sorry I did wrong." The tears dripped onto the quilt as he prayed. "Please forgive me. Lord, forgive me. I wish so badly you'd forgive me, God. Please, please, God. Amen." Then Paul and Al prayed that Aden would become a new child of God and find the freedom and joy of total surrender to God.

After the prayers, they all stood up. Paul asked, "Do you have peace and joy, Aden?"

Aden shook his head. "No, I don't really feel at peace."

"Then why don't we kneel down again, and you should ask God to make you a new person. Ask Him to come into your life and start working," said Paul. The three boys knelt down the second time, and Aden prayed again.

"Lord, forgive me. Help me. I need you. Please forgive me, God. Take my sins away. I do want you to forgive me. I ask that you come into my life. Amen."

Although Aden still didn't feel any different, Paul prayed, "God, thank you so much for forgiving Aden. Thank you for showing him your love. Thank you that he has been delivered from the grips of Satan and that he's now your child. In Jesus' name we pray, Amen."

Suddenly the light of God shone into Aden's heart. While Paul prayed, Aden realized and accepted the fact that God had saved him. He thanked the Lord for salvation. He could feel that deep peace, the kind that can only come from God, penetrate the very core of his heart. His longings for sinful pleasures faded away, as did his other gods. He was wondrously changed by the power of Jesus Christ.

With tears in his eyes, Aden told Al and Paul that he had prayed that very day, "God, if nothing happens today, I'll forget about serving you. I'll go out into the world and stay there."

A buggy full of joy traveled home that night. Tears of gratitude flowed down Paul's cheeks as he and Al marveled at how God changed Aden.

The next day Aden took his idols behind the barn and smashed them to pieces with an axe. He had no more desire to follow the ways of the world and Satan.

Chapter 10
The Foolish Fox

"Love not the world, neither the things that are in the world. If any man love the world, the love of the Father is not in him."
—1 John 2:15

When Paul was seventeen years old, he told the bishop of the church that he would like to be baptized. Paul came to this decision after reading the command in God's Word. After an extended period of instruction, Paul and eight other young people were baptized. A settled peace rested on Paul as he acknowledged before the church, his family, and friends that he would follow and obey God to the best of his abilities.

Although Paul grew in his relationship with Christ, he still found many things in the Bible hard to understand. He loved God even more than when he first became saved; however, many times he had difficult questions with no definite answers. Paul prayed, "God, what would you want me to do in this situation? Is it okay to do this?" Other times he asked, "Should I go to this place tonight or not?" Sometimes Paul asked God about clothing. "Should I wear this? Surely it won't matter, or does it?" He also had a really big question for God: "What is the most important thing you want me to do?"

The pressures from his peers and others around him made Paul struggle with these questions. He didn't know how to view the big and little things—sometimes they seemed harmless. Were they really so?

One day, God showed Paul an important truth.

It was the middle of November, and trapping season had just opened. Paul had never trapped before, but he thought the fur prices were high enough that he'd try to catch a red fox and sell its pelt.

Earlier in the week, Paul had taken the horse and buggy to town. He stopped at the hardware store to look for items for his trap line. He chose some four-inch steel traps, a pair of rubber gloves, and some specially designed stakes. The whole way home he schemed about the best and easiest way to lure a fox.

Now it was Saturday morning, and the traps and stakes were in boiling water on the stove. Paul was standing beside the pot, wearing his new rubber gloves. When the traps and stakes had been boiling long enough to be completely free of human scent, he turned the burner off and carefully lifted the hot traps out of the water. Paul knew foxes were sly, and if their noses caught any human scent, the foxes wouldn't even come close to his traps.

Getting everything ready took a long time. It wasn't until after lunch that Paul gathered his gloves, trap, and stake for his first attempt at catching a fox. He started out the lane when a sudden thought struck him. *How am I going to catch a fox without bait?* He retraced his steps and went to the chicken house. Fortunately, a dead chicken was conveniently lying in the corner. He picked it up and headed out the lane again, thinking, *As ripe as this chicken is, a fox ought to smell it a quarter mile away.* Still smiling to himself, Paul crossed the creek bottom and clambered up the other side. There, along a grassy strip, he carefully chose a spot where he thought a fox would try to cross the creek.

Making sure he was wearing his rubber gloves, Paul dug a small hole in the ground about the size of the dead chicken. He placed the chicken in the hole and covered it partially with dirt. That way the scent of the chicken could escape. Then he carefully dug another hole in front of the chicken, drove a stake deep into the hole, and covered everything with dirt. The only thing sticking out of the dirt was a chain that had one end attached to the stake. Paul attached the other end of the chain to the trap and carefully placed the trap on top of the fresh mound of dirt. Finally he set the trap and sprinkled more dirt, leaves, and grass over the trap's jaws.

As Paul turned to leave, he wondered, *Is that trap concealed well enough? I sure hope so.* He shrugged his shoulders and walked back across the creek bottom and up the other side to the little gravel lane that led back to the house.

The sun cast its last rays across the hills. It was a signal to the roosters to choose their roosting spots for the night. The hens gathered their young

and joined the roosters in the chicken house. The dog's ears became a bit more alert; he was the night watchman of the farm and tonight he would stand guard. Horses in their stalls quietly munched freshly tossed hay. But while the barnyard was quieting down to sleep for the night, a creature of the woods and fields was just waking up.

It was nearly ten o'clock before Paul dared to shine his flashlight across the creek bottom to see whether he could spot anything. The long beam reached the other side. Sure enough! On the other side of the creek was a pair of shining eyes. Paul dashed toward the trap. When he reached the place where he had set the trap, his flashlight shone on a large, handsome red fox.

What was the fox doing? He wasn't eating the chicken. Surely that was why the fox had come to that place, but now, instead of enjoying his meal, he was tugging at the trap with all his might. The fox had forgotten all about the chicken, and was jumping and pulling, twisting round and round to free himself, but there was no way he could get free.

Quickly Paul killed the fox. After making sure the fox was dead, he opened the trap and carried the fox home.

Paul was pleased that the fox hadn't smelled or seen the hidden trap. All those precautions had paid off! After all, Paul was not trying to feed the fox. He wanted to kill it. To trap the fox, though, Paul had to lure him with something tasty, something the fox would enjoy. Otherwise the fox would not have come near the hidden trap.

Late that night, after the fox had been skinned and the pelt hung to dry, Paul reflected on the day's happenings. He thought back to his careful planning, how he had made sure everything was free of his scent, and how he had hidden the trap right in front of that tasty dead chicken. It had worked! He had caught a fox the first night. He smiled to himself in the dim light of the oil lamp.

But suddenly an important truth dawned on Paul's mind, and his face sobered. Satan also was a master of disguise and was carefully hiding his traps. He was luring people into the traps by baiting them with worldly pleasures, entertainment, sports, fashion, and music. Just as Paul had smiled at his success, so Satan was grinning as he successfully trapped and destroyed people—people with eternal souls.

Paul shivered as he visualized this truth. He reached for his Bible and read 1 John 2:15: "Love not the world, neither the things that are in the world." Then he read Galatians 6:14 and learned that he must be crucified unto the world, and the world unto him. *Oh,* Paul thought, *the only way I can avoid being caught in Satan's traps is to die to the world and its attractions. I have to value my relationship with God more than any bait Satan puts in front of me.* So Paul began to ask himself a simple question whenever he was tempted or faced a decision: *What will this do to my relationship with Jesus Christ?* When he answered that question honestly, it helped him make godly choices. It kept him away from Satan's trap.

Chapter 11
Held by a Dark Hand

"The thief cometh not, but for to steal, and to kill, and to destroy: I am come that they might have life, and that they might have it more abundantly."
—John 10:10

Something was not right in Paul's heart. What could it be? Paul mulled over the past day. He had spent the day in the fields helping his uncle. *What did I do? What is it, God? Why don't I feel good?* These questions plagued Paul as he washed up for supper.

Uncle Freeman had come over in the early morning hours and asked Paul to help him find water for a new well. Eagerly Paul grabbed his hat and headed to the barn where he kept the wires he used to find water. Returning to Uncle Freeman's buggy, Paul jumped in, and away they went. The crisp morning air, the *clip-clop* of the horse's hooves, and the beautiful fall weather had a way of making the day seem better. Uncle Freeman and Paul chatted all the way to Uncle Freeman's place, catching up on the latest developments in both households.

"I'm mighty glad you can help me today," Uncle Freeman sighed. "I was getting weary of thinking where the best spot would be for a well. When

Samuel told me you helped him find water down yonder at his place, I thought, *Ah-ha, that's what I'll do. I'll have Paul come and solve my problem.*" Uncle Freeman's eyes twinkled as he spoke.

"Well, I'll try my best, and I hope it's good enough for you." Paul glanced at his uncle from under the brim of his hat.

"Sounds like a plan," Uncle Freeman answered as he guided the horse and buggy alongside his barn. "Whoa there, Sid! Easy!"

The two jumped off the buggy, and after the horse was unharnessed and munching on his grain, Uncle Freeman and Paul made their way past the barn and into the field.

"Now," explained Uncle Freeman, "this is the area where I would like to dig the well, but you just tell me where you find water, and we'll go from there."

Paul surveyed the area. He gripped a wire tightly in each hand and began walking back and forth across the field. On the fourth pass the wires in his hands crossed each other. "Well, looks like we're onto something here," he exclaimed. Paul retraced his steps to the spot where the wires had moved, and again the wires crossed, indicating water.

"Good! Now can you try another spot?" Uncle Freeman asked, scratching his head. "How about over in that direction closer to the house?"

"We can give it a try," Paul said as he marked the spot where he had found water. He made his way through the pasture in the direction Uncle Freeman had pointed.

"By the way," Uncle Freeman asked suddenly,

"how does that work?"

"Well . . . " Paul thought for a moment. "They say it has a lot to do with how much electricity you have in your body."

"Really? That's interesting," Uncle Freeman exclaimed.

"Then there's some kind of magnetic field of energy in the earth that somehow makes it work," Paul continued. "I don't understand the science of it all, but I know it works."

"Well, the way I see it," Uncle Freeman replied, "there's a lot of things this old boy doesn't understand with his limited education, but if it works, that's all I need to know."

"Yeah, that's the way I see it too. If it works it must be okay," Paul agreed.

Paul held his rods in front of him and started walking slowly through the part of the pasture that Uncle Freeman had indicated. Nothing happened. After going about fifty yards, he turned around and slowly zigzagged across the same section. This time the rods moved. Paul stopped and kicked at the dirt to mark the spot. "Well," he asked, "how's this spot?"

"I've just been thinking how that's got to be a better spot," Uncle Freeman said. "Since this part of the pasture is so rugged, we have a hard time keeping the weeds down. Plus, this rise would be perfect for a windmill."

"Yes, I'm sure you would grab a lot more wind here than over yonder," Paul answered as he double-checked to see whether the rods crossed again. "And besides, this is closer to your house, so the trenches won't need to be as long. Less digging means less work for you!"

"Yes, indeed, and I'll take less work any day!" Uncle Freeman chuckled.

"So you feel satisfied with this spot then?" Paul asked.

"Yes, I do. Now how about if we take a little trip to my wife's kitchen and taste her latest creation?"

Paul smiled as he answered, "Uncle Freeman, you should know this boy doesn't turn food down very easily."

"I figured as much," Uncle Freeman replied.

The two walked into the kitchen where Uncle Freeman's wife was busy dishing out some creamed eggs. She looked up and smiled. "Hello, Paul. Come on in and have a seat before these eggs cool off."

"Thank you," Paul said as he washed his hands.

After filling their stomachs, the two men thanked the cook and went out to harness the horse and hitch him to the buggy. As they headed toward home, questions chased each other around Paul's mind. *What is it that doesn't feel right to me?* He glanced at Freeman, who was enjoying the countryside. *Wonder if he feels the same way. Oh, well, it's probably just my imagination.* But Paul's mind kept spinning.

That evening when Paul was lying on his bed reading his Bible, the same uneasy feeling came over him. He felt terrible. The scene of the morning out on the hillside searching for water replayed itself in his mind. It was as though a battle was going on. Paul wasn't sure what it all meant. He mused to himself, *I wonder if there is something wrong with finding water. No, God created me with this extra electricity, so it can't be wrong.*

Paul continued to feel troubled. His Christian life took a downward plunge into turmoil. It seemed God was far away, but why? It just didn't make sense.

After long weeks of confusion, Paul slowly came to the realization that the turmoil must have something to do with the rods and finding water. The scene of walking through Uncle Freeman's field, expectantly holding out those rods, kept flashing in his mind. Paul could not shake the uneasy feeling that something wasn't right about that situation. One night found Paul on his knees out behind the chicken house.

He earnestly prayed, "God, I have no idea why finding water like that could be wrong. I've been doing it for years! I really don't think there's anything wrong with it, but I want to be open to you, so please show me what to do. I need you and I can't live without your peace in my life. I feel hopeless, afraid, and weak. I love you and long for you, O God. In Jesus' name, Amen." Paul stood up and slowly made his way toward the house through the moonlight. A cloud of oppression hung over him in the heavy silence of the night. "I can't see it being wrong, there's no way," he murmured to himself. "But what if there really is something wrong with it?"

By the time Paul reached the house, he had decided to look in God's Word for some answers. The dark hand that kept Paul's peace at bay tightened its grip as he picked up his Bible. This really was a battle, a battle of good against evil and light against darkness.

While searching the Bible, Paul came across some verses in Deuteronomy 18:9–12a. "When thou art come into the land which the Lord thy God giveth thee, thou shalt not learn to do after the abominations of those nations. There shall not be found among you any one that maketh his son or daughter to pass through the fire, or that useth divination, or an observer of times, or an enchanter, or a witch, or a charmer, or a consulter with familiar spirits, or a wizard, or a necromancer. For all that do these things are an abomination unto the Lord."

Paul didn't understand all the words in this passage, so he got out his dictionary and a tattered commentary. What he found troubled him. Necromancy referred to inquiring from the demonic world about things one doesn't know. Divination meant trying to foretell the future. Paul also found that the term "divining rod" was connected to divination. Further research brought him to Hosea 4:12, which read, "My people ask counsel at their stocks, and their staff declareth unto them: for the spirit of whoredoms hath caused them to err, and they have gone a whoring from under their God."

Then it made sense. Sorrow clutched at Paul's heart and tears started welling up in his eyes. He slipped down to his knees and said, "God, I can't believe how sinful I am. I thought I was okay, but now I see the wrong I have done. Would you forgive my wicked heart? Please forgive my sins and give me peace."

What a change was wrought within Paul's heart! He found peace, indescribable and wonderful peace! Now he knew without a doubt that finding water with those rods was sin. No wonder he had lost his peace with God! Yes, it all made sense now. Satan had been using this method to trap Paul and keep him from victory in Jesus.

Paul rose from his knees and slid into bed. As he lay there thinking, he remembered those rods hanging in the barn. Jumping out of bed, he quickly dressed and went out to the barn. There they were, those rods of darkness. Paul shivered just holding them. He prayed over them, rebuking the powers of darkness that had bound him through the rods. Then he threw them on the trash pile. Relief washed over his body and the peace in his soul became even greater. Paul was finally released from the grip of a dark hand.[1]

---

[1] For further research on water witching, read Ken Miller's book, *Dowsing—How Does It Work?* available from Calvary Publications, 11095 Pleasant Hill Rd, Dundee, Ohio, 44624.

Part Three:
Knowing God

Chapter 12
Judith

"The sacrifices of God are a broken spirit: a broken and a contrite heart, O God, thou wilt not despise."
—Palm 51:17

Years went by and Paul grew to manhood. One clear September day he entered a new phase of life. He and his fiancée, Orpha, were married! After the flurry of preparation and the day of the wedding, Paul and Orpha were finally by themselves. Paul felt pure joy as he held Orpha's hand for the very first time. "Orpha," he said, "I can't imagine life much better than this! Let's kneel down and thank the Lord."

"Yes, good idea," Orpha replied, and they knelt down in front of the sofa and dedicated their lives to God.

Life truly was good. The small, rented house on the hillside afforded wonderful times of fellowship. Candle-lit dinners, warm summer nights spent watching the thunderclouds from the front porch swing, and winter walks in the glistening snow all added to their joy. The two worked hard, dreaming of earning enough money for a house to call their own.

Two years later found Paul and Orpha shopping

for a little crib. Spring was fast approaching—and so was the birth of their baby! Paul and Orpha were so excited they could hardly wait.

Judith was born in April. They brought the little girl with ringlets of dark hair around her face home to their little house. It seemed that their baby was picture perfect. How Mama and Daddy loved their little one!

When she was three months old, Judith started crying a lot. She didn't gain weight properly, and her parents couldn't understand what was happening to their little girl. Was it colic, or was she teething? During one such night of fitful sleep, Orpha wearily crawled out of bed once again to tend to her little girl. Tears filled Orpha's eyes. She felt so incapable and at a complete loss. She had no idea what to do for the baby. As Judith cried, her heart-wrenching wails woke up Daddy.

"Here, honey, let me take a turn," Paul said. "You go sleep while I tend to her." He didn't have to say it twice. Orpha climbed under the covers and instantly fell asleep. In the meantime, Paul's mind was full of questions and he tried to pray. "Lord, please help Judith feel better. Make her well, and help us to figure out what's wrong with her."

The ladies at church started talking about little Judith. "I might be wrong, and I sure don't want to tell them, but it's not normal for a baby her age to cry so much," Alta said. She and Rhoda watched out the kitchen window as Paul and Orpha's buggy headed home after church.

"Yes, I've thought about it too," Rhoda acknowledged. "Surely they know something's wrong."

"It sure would be tough knowing what to do." Alta and Rhoda quieted their thoughts as the dishes kept clattering.

Paul and Orpha heard through the grapevine that other people thought their little girl wasn't quite normal. The very idea hurt so much. Paul and Orpha didn't want to accept it just yet. Surely this was just a passing phase in Judith's life; surely she would get over it! Paul and Orpha felt the judgment of others, and it pained their hearts.

Eventually, after days of turmoil, Paul and Orpha began to consider whether the ladies at church really did know what they were talking about.

What if she's handicapped? What are we going to do? Paul's thoughts frightened him. *Why, Lord? Don't you see we want to live pure, godly lives? What have we done wrong to deserve this? I'm trying to serve you and this is what I get? God, you aren't being fair!*

Bitter thoughts flooded Paul's heart as he struggled to accept the reality that his precious little girl might never be a healthy child. *Will she ever come running to me saying, "Daddy, Daddy?"* he wondered. Oh, how he longed to hear her say those words to him.

Judith had no abnormal features that might indicate a developmental problem, but she didn't gain weight or develop her motor skills like the doctors expected. These facts helped Paul and Orpha realize that something really was wrong with Judith.

When Judith was eight months old, Dr. Mullet sent her to a specialist for an evaluation. A whole week's worth of testing—and all the doctors could say was, "We don't know what's wrong, but she'll never be a normal child. Take her home and care for her just like you've been doing." The test results seemed so final and cold. Judith's future didn't look at all promising.

A friend suggested a doctor in Phoenix, Arizona, who might be able to help their daughter. Desperate, Paul and Orpha decided to see this doctor. It took twenty-four hours to reach their destination. The train ride was scenic enough as they passed through vast expanses of wilderness and rode through towns and villages, but Paul and Orpha paid little attention. Judith was irritable and cried until she was so exhausted she fell asleep. "This will be worth it all if the doctor can help her," Paul said, trying to be cheerful, but inside he felt totally helpless and out of control.

When they arrived in Phoenix, Paul asked the hotel manager if he could give him any work to do as pay for their hotel room. Sure enough, early one morning the phone in Paul and Orpha's room rang. It was the hotel manager, asking whether Paul was available to fix a hot water heater. "Sure!" Paul said.

"We'll need it fixed as soon as possible," the hotel manager told him.

"Yes, I'll be right down," Paul said eagerly. The hotel manager found a few other odd jobs for Paul, and Orpha and Judith went to the clinic by themselves that day.

Paul and Orpha made sure Judith was at the clinic every day. They had high hopes, but the treatments at the clinic did nothing. Finally the doctor said, "I've done all I can to help." Paul and Orpha's hopes were dashed again.

An aunt suggested yet another doctor in Des Moines, Iowa. Paul and Orpha scheduled a series of treatments with this doctor. Uncle Paul and his wife Sovilla drove them out to Des Moines in their car. Orpha stayed in Des Moines with Judith while Paul went back home with Uncle Paul and Aunt Sovilla. It was a sad farewell. "Oh, honey, I'm going to miss you so much!" Paul said as he hugged his wife and daughter. Then he got into the car and watched as they faded from his view.

It was a sad and lonely time for Paul. He didn't like being so far from Orpha and Judith, but there were bills to pay, and he felt he must stay home to work. Evenings at home were too silent, and the occasional phone calls weren't frequent enough.

After a month of treatments, Orpha heard the same words that the doctor in Phoenix had told them: "Sorry, we have done all we can." Devastated, Paul again made the trek out to Iowa to bring his beloved wife and daughter home.

Throughout this difficult time it seemed God was far away, oblivious to the cries of a sick little girl and her anxious parents. One night Judith cried for hours until Orpha was crying too. Orpha rocked Judith, sang to her, walked the floor with her, fed her, and changed her, all in an attempt to soothe her to sleep, but nothing helped. In desperation, Paul went outside the house. He fell on his face beside the bushes and wept until he could weep no more. He cried, "Oh, God, where are you? We desperately need you! Don't you hear?" Silence, again. Did God care?

One particularly terrible night, Judith cried from six-thirty in the evening to five o'clock the next morning. Her skin started turning black. Her cries rang through the darkness as she tossed her head back and forth in agony. The scene was almost more than Mama and Daddy could handle. Grandma was there too, and it tore at her heart to see her only granddaughter suffer.

At three o'clock in the morning Paul, Orpha, and Grandma knelt in desperation beside the sofa and poured their hearts out to God. Paul prayed, "Oh, God, I've asked for a miracle. But tonight I give up myself, my life—everything I have is yours, even Judith." Paul wept bitterly as he prayed, "God, you can have her. Take her home! She's yours, Lord. I give her to you."

Orpha sobbed and joined the prayer. "Yes, God, I love her so much, but you can have her now. You gave her to us, but please take her home so she doesn't need to suffer anymore!"

As soon as Paul and Orpha gave Judith to God, her cries stopped. They didn't know whether she had fallen asleep or died, but they kept on praying. Their hearts were broken, but they found peace in total surrender to the will of God.

Paul and Orpha continued praying for two hours, asking God to take their daughter home where there would be no sorrow, no tears, and no pain. They did not want to see Judith die; rather, they wanted to spare her from the pain of living. It was heart-wrenching for them to say, "Lord, we've done all we can. Will you please take her home?"

When Paul and Orpha were done praying, they rose from their knees and tiptoed to Judith's crib. She was breathing peacefully. God had taken her pain away so she could rest. Though they knew they might lose their precious daughter, they now had peace, knowing God's way was best.

Chapter 13
A Mission Without Words

"Confess your faults one to another, and pray one for another, that ye may be healed. The effectual fervent prayer of a righteous man availeth much."
—James 5:16

Another wonderful thing took place on the night Paul and Orpha gave their little girl to God. God had been reminding Paul throughout the years of a sin he had committed ten years earlier. Oh, he had confessed it to God, but Paul hadn't been willing to confess to his brothers and sisters in the church that he had sinned against them. When God broke Paul's heart that night, he was willing to do anything to have peace with God.

Paul wept bitterly as he prayed, "God, I am willing to go back and make things right! I don't care about my reputation anymore. I'll go confess my sin before the church!"

Paul went to work the next morning tired but happy. He thought about how Jacob in the Old Testament had wrestled with God. Paul and Orpha, too, had wrestled with God. Paul also thought about Abraham's willingness to sacrifice his son. The similarities were striking. Paul was willing to sacrifice Judith and had taken her to "Mt.

Moriah," but God had spared her life. God showed Himself strong! What an encouragement to Paul and Orpha's weary hearts.

That evening after Paul came home from work, he looked out the window and saw two sisters from church walking in the lane carrying a basket. The visitors did not say much. They came in, handed the basket to Orpha, and said, "We heard Judith wasn't well, so we brought you some supper." Then they left. It meant so much to Paul and Orpha to have someone care about their trial. They were reminded that God had not forsaken them.

Judith was still a very sick little girl. She maintained a good appetite, but she apparently wasn't getting much nutrition from her food. Slowly she grew thinner and thinner.

Paul confessed his sin to the church, and peace flooded his soul. He wondered why he had put it off for so long. He was certainly thankful he'd had time to make things right. Paul's heart ached, though, with the realization that it had taken Judith, their little "missionary," to help Daddy find freedom.

Judith didn't minister only to Daddy. Many people came to visit and left crying, touched by the suffering they witnessed. Strangers, people Paul and Orpha had never seen before, came to see their family. Judith's tiny life ministered to people no one else on earth could touch.

xxxxx

After much preparation, Paul and Orpha started building a house. When it was partially finished, the family moved into the basement. The house was located on top of a hill only a mile or two from where Orpha's widowed mother lived. That way Orpha's mother could easily help Orpha when the days were long and the nights sleepless. The scenery at their new place was beautiful, but they hardly noticed their surroundings. Judith was the focus of their attention, and she still wasn't healthy.

One day Paul came home from work, set his lunch box down, and walked over to the crib to see Judith. As he stood watching his daughter, who was mere skin and bones by now, he heard a voice say, "Paul! That's you!"

What? he wondered within himself. *How can this be me?*

God said, "You go to church Sunday after Sunday. You're fed and watered by the Word, but you're still starving."

Paul meditated on these words. He felt convicted and saw his wrong. Dropping his head on the crib, he wept. "Oh, God, please forgive me for all the times I've heard your Word, but didn't apply it to my life. For the times I've read the Bible, but didn't feast on its manna. I've stunted my own growth in you! God, I want a deeper walk with you at all costs! All I want is you, Jesus!"

xxxxx

On a day never to be forgotten, Paul left for work early in the morning. Orpha had packed a lunch for him and spent some quiet time with the Lord. Then she started washing the clothes. As she was hanging out the last load of wet laundry, she decided to check on Judith, who was sleeping longer than usual. As Orpha neared Judith's bedroom, she noticed a different sound. It was Judith's breathing, but Orpha had never heard Judith's breathing sound like that. Orpha picked up the baby. She was limp, her breathing slow and raspy. There was no response or even a stirring. Judith seemed to be in a coma.

Since they had no phone, Orpha couldn't call Paul and tell him to come home. What should she do? She did not want to leave Judith to make the call from a phone booth. Feeling frantic, Orpha held her darling close, crying and praying that God would somehow help. Tears dropped down onto the still body in her arms.

Suddenly she heard something. What was that? Did she hear the door squeak upstairs? Or was it just her imagination? The family was still living in the basement and couldn't always hear what was happening on the main floor of the house.

"Paul," she called. No answer. "Yoo-hoo, Paul!"

"Yes," answered a gruff voice. Orpha knew it did not sound like her Paul. "Knock, knock, may I come in?" called the unknown visitor.

"Yes, come in," Orpha said as her shoulders heaved a sigh of relief. In walked Cousin Paul, wanting to talk to her husband. What a coincidence—no, providence—from God!

"Oh, I'm so glad you came," Orpha gasped. "There's something wrong with Judith. Could you please find Paul and tell him to come home right away?"

"I sure can," was Paul's astonished reply. "I'll find him. Don't worry." With that the messenger bounded up the stairs out of the basement, slamming the door behind him. Again all was silent except for little Judith's labored breathing.

It seemed like hours until the door burst open and Paul rushed in. He hurried over to where Orpha was rocking their baby. His arms gently encircled the two as his head fell over the little girl. There the two parents wept, for they knew Judith's departure was near.

A soft knock sounded and Grandma came in. More and more people gathered. Neighbors, aunts, uncles, and friends entered the room. They stood in a circle around the little family, praying and weeping together.

Orpha was able to hold the baby for forty-five minutes before Judith took one long, last breath. During that last breath, a single tear slipped out of one closed eye and coursed its way down her little cheek. Life had fled. The little missionary's life was over, but her legacy lived on, speaking to those around her and stirring their hearts. Judith had cried a lot, but only twice did she have tears: once when she hit her head and once when she shed a tear of farewell. It was as though she said, "Farewell, Mama and Daddy, Grandma, friends . . . I have to go now."

God ministered to Paul and Orpha in numerous ways after Judith's death. That farewell tear would always be a treasured memory. The people who attended Judith's viewing were encouraging and supportive. One older man came through the line, sat down beside Paul, and put his hand on Paul's knee. "Paul," the man said, "I have a son whom I would gladly lay down in her stead if only he would be living right." With tears in his eyes he continued, "Praise the Lord that you have no doubt where she is now!" The man stood up and continued down the line, leaving Paul with words that made a lasting impression.

"Yes," Paul acknowledged to himself, "I have pain, but that older man's pain is much deeper than mine!"

As Paul and Orpha stood weeping by the tiny casket, the goodbyes seemed so final. Just before the lid of the casket was closed, Paul reached into his suit coat and pulled out his special Bible. Though that Bible meant a lot to him, Paul laid it beside Judith as a symbol that God's Word would be with her. Then the final click of the lid was heard, separating Mother and Father from their little girl until they, too, entered eternity.

During Judith's short life, she never sat by herself and never rolled over. All she could do was lift her tiny head off the pillow. She cried more than many adults do in a lifetime. But though she had been so helpless, the things her daddy learned through her life changed the direction of his. The little missionary had accomplished her mission and completed her journey. She was buried in a cemetery up on the hillside about a mile from home. On her gravestone they inscribed, "A Mission Without Words."

Chapter 14
Fuel Tank Miracle

"Trust in the Lord with all thine heart;
and lean not unto thine own understanding."
—Proverbs 3:5

P aul and Orpha's life changed after Judith died. Judith's fussiness and ill health had prevented them from attending church together as a family. Now they could go to church together, but with empty, aching arms and hearts. After services were over, they would return home to a quiet but painfully empty house. Slowly their lives found a new normal as they grieved and adjusted to losing their precious baby Judith.

Two years later, Paul and Orpha welcomed a robust, healthy baby girl into their home. It seemed as though little Julia brought healing into a home of sorrow. Giggles and laughter filled the rooms where death and sadness had visited two years before. Paul and Orpha's aching hearts found both a balm and a blessing in the miracle of their new daughter.

Another two years went by, and Paul and Orpha began attending a conservative Mennonite church. A year after that, Paul started working at a new company as a commercial refrigeration technician.

Soon he was promoted to the position of service manager. Paul loved his job. There were a lot of challenges in the business world, but he found his work very fulfilling. Life was good, the pay was more than ample, and Paul was satisfied.

Then an opportunity came for Paul to work with Christian Aid Ministries, a nonprofit charitable organization that channeled funds from conservative Anabaptist groups to needy people in various countries. Paul struggled with knowing what God was asking him to do. Should he leave the business world and become involved in full-time ministry? How would he take care of his family? Paul was faced with a grave decision, one that would alter his life forever. In his mind he argued, *God, you know I have a terrible fear of flying, and this type of ministry always involves travel. Surely this can't be your will. What if I die overseas and leave my family behind?* After a year and a half of struggle and losing sleep, Paul dedicated himself to obedience at all costs. He decided to enter full-time ministry.

Paul had spent five and a half years at a job he enjoyed. When he left his business office for the last time, he drove away weeping and said, "God, I don't understand, but I'm coming your way. You will need to take care of my family!"

Jesus had come to Paul's "Sea of Galilee" and said, "Follow me!" Paul had his fishing nets in order, was making good money and enjoying his life and career, but how could he argue with God? Trusting God wasn't easy; however, Paul came to the conclusion that being in the center of God's will is always the best place to be, even though sometimes the cost is great. Paul was beginning to understand Jesus' call to the fishermen. "And Jesus, walking by the sea of Galilee, saw two brethren, Simon called Peter, and Andrew his brother, casting a net into the sea: for they were fishers. And he saith unto them, Follow me, and I will make you fishers of men" (Matthew 4:18-19).

For Paul, one of the costs of being in God's will was that he had to face his fear of flying. In 1987 Paul boarded an airliner on one of his first transatlantic flights. He was bound for the communist country of Romania. His apprehension mounting, Paul took a deep breath and desperately prayed. "Please help me to trust you, God. I need you here with me each step of the way. I don't know whether I'll see my family again, but I want to trust you. Forgive me for my lack of faith, and give me a safe trip to Romania."

When Paul opened his eyes, the huge jet was taxiing out to the runway. As Paul watched the ground crew working and other planes taxiing in, his mouth suddenly dropped open. There, on the engine of the aircraft, perched a white dove! The bird was trying hard to stay balanced against the engine's vibrations and the bumps of the plane over the pavement. The dove's tail feathers bobbed up and down, and occasionally it flapped its wings as it tried to stay on the engine. When the plane slowed just before takeoff, the white dove flew straight toward Paul's window and spread its wings to land.

Paul craned his neck to follow the bird's path, but it was nowhere to be seen. Then God whispered to

Paul, "I am with you, and the safest place for you is in the center of my will. Trust me. I know your future. I know your fears. I can take care of everything!" Paul always remembered that lesson on trust.

The plane safely arrived in Amsterdam, Holland, eight hours later. The next flight to Vienna, Austria, was also trouble-free, and from Vienna, Paul and those with him rented a car and drove to Romania to visit Christian contacts.

The group consisted of Paul, David Troyer (Paul's friend and coworker), and two other men involved in helping needy Christians in Romania. The men made their way to a pastor's house in Alexandria, a city in the southern part of the country. This was to be the first stop of their weeklong trip. To appear inconspicuous, the men drove purposefully toward Alexandria and did not loiter to look at the scenery as they might have done.

Before leaving Vienna, each man had memorized a portion of the pastor's address and phone number. They also memorized specifics like house color, fence color, gate color, which door to enter upon arrival, and where to park their vehicle. They knew they needed to take every precaution to spare the pastor's life and keep his family from further hardships. Any unusual occurrence at any given house was likely to be voiced to the secret police, who would then interrogate and harass whomever they found at the house, especially the father or the pastor of a church. Many pastors were in prison for their faith. Others had died in their quest to remain true to God and His Word.

By late afternoon Paul and the others had arrived in the little town of Alexandria. They found their way down the right street and saw a green fence surrounding a small cottage. "That's it!" exclaimed David.

The men tried to take in all the details without arousing suspicion. Then they left the area, parked the car in another part of the city, and returned on foot to the little cottage with the green fence. When they reached the cottage, they walked right in without knocking, as though they had entered the cottage a thousand times. Of course, they had never even seen this place before!

Inside, the pastor's wife welcomed them with tears of gratefulness. Her son interpreted for her. "I'm sorry," she said. "My husband is not here now, but he will be back tomorrow."

Just then they all heard a car skid to a stop outside the cottage. One of the boys came running in and said, "Shhh! *Politzia, Politzia.* Hide quickly!" The children and their mother quickly pulled every shade in the cottage and muffled the telephone in case the police had tapped the line. They motioned the visitors into a little room and silently shut the door behind them. Just then there was a loud knocking at the front door.

"Who are those foreigners in your house?" a tall, burly policeman demanded, stepping through the door the pastor's wife had opened. "What do they want? Where do they come from?"

"They are just friends of ours who stopped in to visit," the pastor's wife answered nonchalantly.

"Humph!"

"Where's your husband?" asked another policeman.

"He is out working," she answered.

"We'll be back when he's home!" they half shouted, glaring at the brave little woman.

"Yes, yes! I'll tell my husband you stopped by."

The two policemen shook their heads and mumbled to each other as they walked to their car.

After waiting a few minutes, the pastor's wife slowly opened the door and motioned the men out of the room. In broken English, the pastor's son tried to explain his mother's concerns. "We desperately need Bibles, five Christian families, sad, sad. They have little food. Secret police ask about our activities. They take Papa to police headquarters once. Next time they say you go straight to prison." The hours slipped by as they conversed in muffled tones. It became apparent that helping the struggling Christians of Romania would be difficult and required careful planning.

Darkness fell over the city of Alexandria. With tear-filled eyes, the visitors bade farewell to the pastor's wife and family. They shared one last prayer together. Then the men threaded their way through the darkened streets to their car.

Remembering that the fuel light in the car had come on just before they had reached the pastor's house, they immediately began looking for a fuel station as they puttered out of the side streets and onto the main thoroughfare. They soon saw a fuel station ahead and stopped, but the attendant said,

119

"No more." Ten miles later, to their relief, they reached another fuel station. Paul hopped out of the car to speak to the attendant, but the man at the pump shook his head and motioned them to continue down the highway.

"What are we going to do if we can't find any fuel?" David wondered.

"We sure don't want to run out," Paul replied, "but there's no way we'll make it to our hotel without fueling up. We've got at least 75 miles back to the hotel, don't you think?"

"That's just it, and we don't want to risk being caught by the secret police," David said as he gazed at the fuel gauge. "We don't want to answer any questions about why we are here, because that would mean trouble for us and our contacts."

Paul looked ahead and suddenly shouted, "Stop! Stop!"

David slammed on the brakes and the car skidded to a halt mere inches from a passing train. Beside the road they could barely make out the shadowy figure of a man who was frantically waving a dim warning light.

Deeply shaken, they continued toward Bucharest. Again they stopped at a fuel station, and again they got the same response, "Sorry, all gone."

The gravity of their situation was foremost in their weary minds. They all decided to pray for God's help. "Heavenly Father, you know our problem. You know our fears. We need you to help us right now. Help us fill our fuel tank so we can make it to the hotel. We know you have brought us this far in safety and you can safely take us home. We give our lives to you and ask you for a miracle. In Jesus' name, Amen."

Paul looked up and glanced at the fuel gauge. Just like that, the fuel light went off. Before anyone had a chance to speak, the needle on the fuel gauge slowly rose to point at a quarter tank. The men stared at the needle in wonder. They were at a complete loss for words. God was riding with them, and He had just put fuel in their tank. It was an absolute miracle!

"Praise the Lord, and thank you, Jesus," David murmured as he shifted into fifth gear.

"You know what?" Paul asked enthusiastically. "We can trust God! If we are doing His will, we can trust Him. He will help us!"

Chapter 15
Deliverance for Pierre

"But now in Christ Jesus ye who sometimes were far off are made nigh by the blood of Christ."
—Ephesians 2:13

The airport terminal was crowded. People were milling around, waiting for their flights. But not Paul. He was a mere black streak, high-tailing it for his gate. His shoes pounded the floor.

"Last call for flight 1350 heading for Port-au-Prince, Haiti," came the announcement over the loudspeaker. Paul ran even faster. *Almost there! Oh, I hope I make it! Dear Lord, please help me!*

As he ran up to Gate 5, the lady at the desk said, "Oh, are you Paul?"

"Yes, can you get me on the plane?" Paul gasped, chest heaving as he tried to catch his breath.

The lady was already on the phone, conversing with the flight crew. She nodded at Paul and clanked the receiver down. Grabbing her key ring, she headed for the door with Paul close behind. After unlocking the door for him, she grinned and said, "That was as close a call as you'll ever get, sir!"

Paul thanked her and hurried down the jet bridge and into the airplane. Once in his seat, he tried to huff and puff discreetly as the aircraft headed out the runway. He closed his eyes and prayed before takeoff, just as he always did since his very first flight to Romania. *Thank you, Father, for helping me, and may your protecting hand be over this aircraft, the pilots, and the engines. Cover me with your blood. Thank you, Jesus. Amen.*

Upon arrival in Port-au-Prince, Paul waited until the shoving and pushing died down before getting his carry-on and heading out of the airplane. The passengers' mentality seemed to be, "First come, first serve."

Paul's stay was filled with meetings, stressful decisions, and a bit of travel. One of his most memorable trips was to the little village of Zabo, hidden up in the mountains.

The Jeep in which Paul was riding rocked and jerked in all directions until everything seemed to rattle. Even Paul's joints felt sore from all the jolts. It was not a pleasant drive at all! But it had been decided that James Mullet, the American field director for Christian Aid Ministries; Eris Labady, a Haitian interpreter; and Paul would make the bumpy trip to this remote village. Christian Aid Ministries had already rented a storage building in Zabo, but the men needed to find a larger building to store the huge amounts of food that would eventually be distributed to the nearby schools.

They really hoped to find a larger storage building in Zabo itself, because many of the schools were located in the mountains of that area. There were either no roads at all leading to the schools, or else the roads were too dangerous for the delivery trucks to traverse. From this little outpost in Zabo, workers would load the schools' shipments of rice and beans on the backs of donkeys. The animals were sure-footed and able to go where the big delivery trucks couldn't.

The three men noticed something was happening as soon as they reached the section of Zabo where the current storage building was located. A dozen or so donkeys were tied to the tall palm trees growing beside the path. A crowd of people milled around, apparently watching someone who was sitting on a chair in the middle of the circle. Eris walked up to the group and asked one of the men, "What's going on here?"

"We're from a village two miles farther up the mountain," the man explained. "This boy from our village went wild, screaming and running as fast as he could. We finally caught up with him here in Zabo. The boy is acting so strange. We think the evil spirits are not happy with him and his family. His father is a voodoo worshiper and practices many things at home."

"How old is the boy and what is his name?" Eris asked.

"He's fourteen, and his name is Pierre," piped up a lady who overheard the question.

"Why are the Catholic priests here?" Eris wondered.

"Well," replied the man, "some people thought he might have a demon inside, so they called the priests to exorcize the demon, but the priests couldn't do anything."

Eris went over to where the boy was sitting. "What's wrong, Pierre?" he asked. "Can you tell me?"

The boy's blank stare was the only answer.

"Do you want to pray?" Eris asked.

Still no answer. Pierre appeared to be dumb.

"Then I'll pray for you," Eris said. He shut his eyes and prayed, "God, would you please help this young boy? Heal him, and make him well."

Nothing happened. Pierre couldn't talk. He had a glassy stare and seemed oblivious to what was happening around him.

Eris went back to James and Paul and explained what was happening.

As the men turned to leave, God spoke quietly to Paul, "Here's a boy who needs help! Is your God not big enough to deliver him? Does this boy need to spend the rest of his life in bondage?"

Paul turned to Eris and said, "God seems to be telling me that we should lay hands on this boy and pray in the name of Jesus."

"Really, Brother Paul? Then let's do it!" Eris said emphatically. Instead of leaving, the men returned to where Pierre was still sitting.

Eris and Paul laid their hands on Pierre. Both men prayed, Eris in Creole and Paul in English. "O God, in the name of Jesus we resist these powers of darkness that are binding Pierre. In the name of Jesus we command these demons to flee."

As soon as the men used Jesus' name to command the powers of darkness to leave Pierre, the donkeys that were tied to the palm trees went wild. They strained at their ropes, braying and stomping. They swished their tails in a frenzy. Pierre, on the other hand, started talking sensibly. The power of Jesus' name had caused the demons to leave Pierre. What an awesome miracle!

"What happened to me?" Pierre asked.

"You were delivered from demons," Eris explained. "Listen, son, unless you allow Jesus Christ to fill your life, those demons will continue to haunt you. What you need is Jesus living inside you!"

"Yes," Pierre murmured. He laid his head on the back of the chair and began weeping.

"Pierre," Eris said, gently tapping his shoulder, "Do you want Jesus to change your life?"

"Yes!" Pierre said, as he looked Eris straight in the eye.

Pierre gave his heart to God and was born again that day.

Two years later Paul was asked to preach a message titled, "Spiritual Warfare and Deliverance Through Christ" at the little Zabo church. After the service a young man came up to him and asked, "Do you recognize me?"

Paul looked at the young man and thought. "Yes," he said after a moment. "Are you Pierre?"

With a shy grin, Pierre answered, "Yes, I am." Through the translator, he added, "I am in instruction class here at this church and will be baptized, Lord willing, in a week." Paul's heart rejoiced in the power of the name of Jesus that had saved and kept Pierre.

Chapter 16
From the Gutter to God

"Quench not the Spirit."
—1 Thessalonians 5:19

The bus pulled out of the church parking lot and onto the road. It was four o'clock in the morning, and every seat was filled and all the luggage stowed. After a brief prayer to God for protection, most of the passengers tried to get a few hours of sleep as the bus headed for New York City.

It was rather odd that these country folk would even dare face the crowds, lights, and skyscrapers of New York City. But a common goal brought them here: a burden for lost souls.

When they reached the heart of the city, the bus parked near Washington Park and everyone got out. Someone preached and the group sang and passed out Gospel tracts on Times Square until close to midnight.

At last the weary travelers found their way to Carter Hotel, an old brick structure infested by cockroaches and other small creatures. Carter Hotel was located on one of Manhattan's most notorious streets. The hotel rooms were not very clean, but at least there were showers and beds for everyone. Getting to sleep was no problem—everyone was so tired.

Paul, Chris, and Mark wearily entered their room on the fifth floor. They were getting ready for bed when Paul stopped them by saying, "We really should pray before we sleep." Chris and Mark agreed. They all knelt, a little afraid they would fall asleep on their knees from exhaustion.

The men prayed, "Oh, Father, there are so many lost people in this city. May you touch the lives and hearts of the homeless, the drug addicts, and the drunks. May your Word spread abroad like a fire and spread your Gospel for your glory. Change the sinful hearts of these men and women. May we be your servants."

As they kept praying, the three men began praying for their own hearts. A revival took place in that dirty hotel room. Each one wept before the Lord and confessed his sins, his stubborn pride, and his selfish desires. Oh, how they needed God afresh and anew! And they found God after their hearts were broken before Him. It was a hallowed time, a sacred time of cleansing and opening up the parts of their hearts that were stained. "God," each was saying, "I give it all up, and I ask your blood to cover my sins."

Here they were in New York City, bringing the Gospel to the lost, and they themselves needed the Gospel! That night they focused on their own hearts, and each could sense the wonderful working of God in his life.

After prayer, the men lay on their beds, but they weren't tired anymore. By now it was Sunday morning. Chris commented, "It's amazing how the power of God can wake a person up in more than one way."

"That's right," said Mark, "The peace I feel inside should make me sleep better than ever, if only I could fall asleep!"

As Paul smiled in the darkness, he felt the softest of nudges in his spirit. "Paul, you need to go out there. Someone needs you." Paul's eyes opened wide. At first he thought it was just his imagination. Then he heard it again. "Paul, someone on the street needs you."

"Are you still awake?" Paul's voice was hushed in the stillness of the room.

"Yes," Chris and Mark responded together.

"Well, somehow I'm sensing that someone out on the street needs us. Do any of you feel the same way?" Paul asked.

"Yes," said Chris as he sat up in bed. "I've sensed the same thing."

"Me too!" echoed Mark.

The men got up and slipped into their wrinkled clothes. They unlocked the door and silently walked down the hallway to the elevator. When it arrived at their floor, they stepped into the little cabin that creaked and swayed and finally jerked to a halt at ground level. The doors slid open and the three men walked past the front desk. They swung open the front door of the hotel and stepped out onto the street. What a dangerous time to be out—it seemed positively reckless! This was New York City, after all, and this very street was notorious for theft, prostitution, and murder. Gangs roamed the city like spiders crawling across their webs, entangling others in their grip. What was God thinking? It was around one-thirty in the morning, a dangerous hour, yet God's voice was plain. "Someone needs you!"

They stood in front of Carter Hotel and wondered if this person would be coming to them for help, or if they should go find him.

A few people passed by. The men hesitated for fifteen minutes, silently asking God to show them where to go. Then God spoke to all three men at once and said, "Go left."

So they turned left and headed down the street. They came to the next street corner, and again God said, "Go left." The three walked quickly. Each was praying silently, sensing a cloud of spiritual darkness in the area.

"O God, cover us with your blood, and help us know and understand your will," Paul quietly prayed as they walked up to yet another street corner.

Again God said, "Go left." Now they were on Broadway Avenue. As they trudged on, they saw two homeless people huddling on the grate across the street. It was the middle of September, and the nights were cool. The grate provided a bit of warmth to the homeless people. Without a word, Paul, Mark, and Chris crossed Broadway and walked up to the motionless forms on the grate. They knew without a doubt their mission was here.

Paul knelt down to look at the figures on the

grate. As he did so, he recognized one of them. It was Little Albert, a man they had met several years before on another witnessing trip to New York City. Albert was absolutely filthy. The stench reached the three men but did not deter them. Paul gently shook the still form and asked, "Albert, is that you?"

"Yes," came his gravelly voice as he raised his head to see who was speaking to him. Paul noticed Albert's long, oily hair that was twisted and tangled together. A thin, dirty blanket covered Albert's body.

"Albert, we came to tell you about Jesus Christ. Would you like to hear about Him?" Paul asked, placing his hand on Albert's shoulder.

"Yes," Albert said as he sat up.

Paul and Chris explained the message of salvation. "You need Christ in your heart to change your life," Chris said.

"Yes," Paul added. "He is the only one who can take you from the gutter of sin and give you new life. Would you like a new life?" Paul asked. "Would you like to become born again and ask Jesus to come into your life?"

"Oh, yes, yes!" Albert replied.

There on Broadway, on top of a rusty grate, under flashing lights and glistening signs, four men knelt while Albert became a changed man. He confessed his sins to the Lord. Big tears rolled down his face that night as he prayed. Most nights he was high on drugs or drunk beyond reason. Not tonight! Tonight Albert knew he had found God.

The first thing he did when he stood up was to

pull his hair away from his face. Albert smiled. It was a big, wide smile. It was a beautiful smile!

The four men walked back to the hotel. They got a room for Albert, who was ecstatic. "I don't remember the last time I slept in a real bed. This is wonderful!" he exclaimed.

"We'll wake you up around seven o'clock," Paul said. "Then you can take a shower and by seven-thirty we'll stop by. We can have breakfast together."

"Sounds good," Albert said. "Thank you so much." With that they closed the door and parted for the night.

"What would have happened if we hadn't given our lives in full surrender and brokenness to the Lord?" Chris asked as they slipped under the covers for the second time.

Paul shook his head in the darkness. "I'm afraid nothing would have happened."

"You know, it really grieves me to think how often I've hindered the Holy Spirit's work in my life because of not being totally surrendered to Him," Mark mused.

"Me too!" said Paul. "Oh, Lord, forgive us."

The next morning at seven-thirty when they knocked on Albert's door, he was ready to go. There was a glow on his face as he raised his hands high and said, "Praise God! Hallelujah!

"You know what I thought of last night as I was lying in that bed?" Albert asked, not waiting for a reply. "If you would have come a half hour earlier last night, you wouldn't have found me. I had just come from Central Park and laid down fifteen minutes before you all came."

"Really?" Mark asked. "So that's why we didn't know which way to go for fifteen minutes."

"Isn't that amazing!" Paul exclaimed as they headed for the elevator.

After breakfast followed by a church service at the Bowery Mission, Albert went with the group as they visited Washington Park one last time before they returned home. Albert passed out tracts and talked with people, telling them what God had done in his life. "Paul, you need to come over here," Albert said, pulling Paul's hand. "My stepfather is over here, and he needs the Lord."

Albert and Paul walked over to where a man sat hunched over. "Pap, listen to me," Albert said, gently shaking the man. "Jesus saved me. He changed my life last night. I'm a new person now. That's what you need!" The man stared straight ahead, his eyes glazed over. He didn't understand. It was so sad.

A few years later on another New York City witnessing trip, Paul checked up on Little Albert. He was still faithful to the Lord and attended the Times Square Church.

Chapter 17
Lost in the Woods

"Take heed to yourselves, that your heart be not deceived, and ye turn aside, and serve other gods, and worship them."
—Deuteronomy 11:16

Paul spent some time training to become an emergency medical technician. He felt God leading him to this volunteer work. More than saving physical lives, he wanted to help hurting men and women find God. Being an EMT was rewarding work. Many times Paul had the chance to ask people if they were ready to meet the Lord.

On one of his first squad calls to a nursing home, Paul had to use the Heimlich maneuver on an older woman who was choking. He wrapped his arms around the woman and suddenly tightened them, helping her get a quick rush of air through her windpipe. Everyone was pleasantly surprised when Ms. Milmont's hot dog flew out of her mouth with such force that it hit the dining room wall.

Yes, occasionally there was laughter, but most times there was pain and agony—and sometimes death.

Paul had been an EMT for almost a year, when one brisk morning he learned an important lesson on the seriousness of deception. He was sitting at his desk when his pager went off. "Attention, East Holmes squad and fire personnel," the dispatcher announced. "You're needed in the vicinity of County Road 172 for a missing person."

Paul slung his jacket over his shoulder and rushed out the door. He was the first one at the station, so he opened the overhead garage door and quickly drove the squad vehicle out of the station. Minutes later the others arrived and the crew of four was on its way.

When they pulled into the farmyard, they found a large crowd of around 200 people who had gathered already. Neighbors, friends, family, firefighters, police, and rescue workers all wanted to help. The police force was in charge of the rescue operation.

An officer told everybody about Glen, the missing person.

Glen had lived on the farm for years. Although he was now an older man and hadn't farmed for several years, his hands still bore the marks of hard labor. He loved the farm: the smell of freshly mown hay, the sound of the windmill pumping water, and the hum of his beloved John Deere tractor.

The previous afternoon, Glen's daughter had come to the house to check on her dad and see whether he needed anything. She stepped into the house with her usual "Hello!" and Glen called back from his favorite blue rocking chair, "Hello, come in!"

"Hi, Dad," she said. "I just thought I'd check on you. I'm going to town and wondered whether you need anything."

"Yeah," Glen replied slowly, "I'll be needing some more food. Cereal . . . bananas . . . maybe some more milk."

"That's all?" his daughter asked.

"You check my refrigerator and then just get what you think." In a mumble he added, "I sure wonder who took my billfold."

"What did you say, Dad?"

"I can't find my billfold anywhere, I said."

"Oh, don't worry, I'll pay for it," she said. "Now Dad, I'll go to town and come back as soon as I've got your groceries. Is that okay?"

"Yes, but where did that go?" Glen continued to mumble to himself as his daughter closed the door softly behind her.

Sighing, she thought, *He's such a dear father! Why does he have to have Alzheimer's disease?*

Although he was still in the beginning stages of Alzheimer's, Glen just could not remember many things anymore. He was still able to live alone, but his family was already starting to put together a plan for his care, because they knew his condition was getting worse.

A little later when Glen's daughter opened the back door with her arms full of groceries, the house was so quiet she thought her dad must be asleep. She peeked into the living room, but no one was there. She searched the whole house without finding him, and then she thought, *Oh well, I should've known! He's in the barn.* The daughter searched every nook and cranny in the entire barn but still didn't find Glen. By then she was truly anxious and worried that someone may have kidnapped her dad. She called 911 and explained her situation. The sheriff and his deputies came to the farm and searched everywhere. No Glen. The local fire department was dispatched, but Glen still was not found. The police called off the search at eleven o'clock that night with plans to resume the following morning.

So now Paul and his squad crew had joined the other searchers at Glen's farm.

"The man is around six feet tall, broad-shouldered, and stoops when walking," a policeman said as he gave Paul and his crew a map of the area. "We have no idea what he's wearing or where he might be."

The policeman used the map to show the crew a large wooded area on the back of the farm where they would search. The crew began peering behind every tree and beside every log. Paul opened the creaky door of an old farrowing house and called, "Glen, do you hear me?"

No answer.

Had Glen suffered a heart attack? Nobody knew what had happened to him, but the searchers needed to be ready for anything. As Paul topped a hill, he finally heard what he was hoping to hear. A faint voice on his radio said, "Attention, all search and rescue personnel. We've found the missing person."

When they had gathered back in the yard, a firefighter told everyone how he had found Glen. "I was walking through the woods on the west side of the farm. I was looking all over, behind brush and around trees, when suddenly a voice behind

me said, 'What are you looking for?' I jumped and turned around, and there was Glen sitting on a stump. I had just passed it; it was about twenty yards to my right. I couldn't believe I had missed him. I said, 'We're looking for you. You are lost!'

"Glen just chuckled and said, 'I'm not lost.'

"I said, 'You have been out here all night. Don't you see you are out here in the woods?' I pointed at the trees. 'And it's cold.'

"He looked around and said, 'I'm not outside; I'm home.'

"I felt his hands and they were as cold as ice. 'Glen, you are cold!' I exclaimed.

" 'No, I'm not cold,' he said very emphatically.

"Then I got on my radio and said, 'I found Glen, and we will need a squad.' We had a terrible time trying to get him on the stretcher. We actually ended up strapping him to the backboard. And even then he was trying to get up." The firefighter shook his head as he concluded, "I just can't believe I walked right past him. I'm glad he hollered at me, or we might never have found him alive."

When Paul got back to his office, he could not stop thinking about Glen.

Because he had Alzheimer's disease, Glen didn't know his true condition. He didn't know he was lost in the woods and sitting on a stump all night. Glen thought he was at home. What's more, because Glen didn't think he was lost, it prevented him from being found. His deception kept him from knowing his true condition. What a sad way to live!

The spiritual parallel burdened Paul's heart

more as the day progressed. *Hmm,* he thought, *there are so many people who are lost, just like Glen. They think they know where they're going, but they have "spiritual Alzheimer's disease," which is deception. They have lost their ability to know their true condition. They think they are going home, but they are lost . . .* "Oh, Lord, may I never forget this lesson, and keep me from deception. Help me to be honest about my relationship with you! Help me to love the truth so my heart will never become hard when I lose my ability to know my true condition."

Chapter 18
Touched by God

"And he said, My presence shall
go with thee, and I will give thee rest."
–Exodus 33:14

P aul had worked hard all day. When he came
home to his family, they all piled into the car.
They were going to Paul's parents' place for
supper! Paul had "ordered" his favorite meal from his
mom's kitchen: Henry's Good Stuff. The ingredients
included brown gravy, dandelions, potatoes, and
hard-boiled eggs. And when topped with fresh, diced
onions . . . mmm, it was most delicious!

Around eleven o'clock that night the family was
finally heading home. Paul was exhausted and
ready to retire for the night, but as he topped the
last hill, he noticed a car parked in their drive. It
belonged to Ben, a young man who was struggling
in his Christian life. On occasion he would come
over to talk to Paul when he needed a listening ear
or some advice.

How can I help him when I'm this tired? Paul
yawned as he lifted his sleeping two-year-old son
into his arms and took him into the house.

Wearily he stepped back out into the warm

summer night. The stars were twinkling overhead. Paul shook Ben's hand and said, "Good evening, Ben. The Lord has given us a beautiful night!"

"That's for sure," Ben replied, "and I'm sorry to bother you, but I just felt I needed to talk."

"Well, I want to be here for you," Paul said, hiding another yawn.

Ben wiped his brow and said, "I just felt too restless to sleep tonight. I have been struggling with these temptations, and it's been robbing me of my peace and joy. I know there is a way of holiness that leads to life. But why can't I live victoriously and claim the peace and joy of God?"

"That is a good question, Ben. I know I have had those times too," Paul said, staring off into the night sky. "I haven't always lived a life of peace and joy. God needs to have total control in order for that to happen. I clearly remember the night I gave my life to God. I have never been the same since! I praise His name for lifting me out of that miry, sticky clay and giving me hope beyond the grave."

Ben stood silently as Paul continued. "It didn't stop there. He took me through some of the bitterest trials and roughest waters to break my stubborn will. He was the one leading me, but I was the one who had to say, 'I give up.' And when I said that, He took over. Oh, bless His name!"

"That's wonderful to hear, but I can't say I've been feeling any joy," Ben responded. "It feels as though a cloud of darkness hangs over me."

"Why don't we pray?" Paul said.

"Yes," Ben replied. "I'd like that."

After the men prayed, Paul shared more of what God had done in his life. Suddenly a brilliant light shone down on the two men. It was radiance itself! It was glory! The men looked up and fell to their knees as one and started praying. "God, we are but dust in your presence, filthy, worthless rags of ourselves. Oh, God, fill us afresh with your holiness. Forgive our unbelief, our self-righteousness, and our pride."

They continued praying. The light still encircled them as their hearts crumbled before God, and they knew without a doubt that this light was the glorious presence of God. Paul and Ben knelt on holy ground, they knew, because God had manifested His divine glory and majesty.

The light shone for about an hour as the two men prayed and sought the face of God. Then the light went away.

Paul wasn't tired anymore; in fact, he wondered whether he would sleep at all that night. Ben, though not normally an emotional person, was filled with feelings of hope, peace, comfort, and rest. And he had joy unspeakable! The glory of God's presence had lifted Ben out of his darkness. That glorious light was a tremendous encouragement to him even though he had been expecting nothing like it. After praising God and thanking Him for manifesting His glory, the two men said their goodbyes.

A little while later, a knock sounded on the door. Paul opened it to find a sheepish Ben. "Brother Paul, sorry to bother you again! I was rejoicing and praising God for showing me His glory, and then I started my car and yanked it into gear so hard I broke the shifter right off."

Laughing, the two men headed out toward the car. After a few futile attempts at fixing it, Ben decided to drive the car home in first gear. In his relationship with God, however, Ben was in high gear. The power and glory of God had changed his life completely!

Chapter 19
Another Mission
Without Words

"And they that were ready went in with him to the marriage: and the door was shut."
—Matthew 25:10

A nother little girl was born to Paul and Orpha. Shana Faith came in the middle of summer. The four older siblings were delighted to see their new little sister. Shana seemed to be the perfect baby! She had a head full of black hair, a lusty cry, and a hearty appetite. What more could they want?

Three weeks later the scenario had changed. Shana still had her curly black hair, but she cried most of the time and didn't gain any weight. This was all too familiar to Paul and Orpha. Did Shana suffer from whatever illness had caused Judith's death?

Every time Shana had a well-baby exam, her doctor told Orpha, "Oh, don't worry, she's just colicky." This made Orpha feel better, but she still wondered if that was the only problem. The weeks passed slowly, none better than the last. Shana cried in her swing, she cried in her bed, and she cried when she was rocked. Nothing seemed to calm her, and finally, exhausted, Shana would cry herself to sleep.

At Shana's five-month checkup, Orpha told the doctor, "I *know* there's something wrong with my baby."

"What makes you say that?" the doctor asked.

"Well, for one thing, she cries so much," Orpha explained. "She doesn't make any eye contact. She rolls over, but other than that she is not developing the way she should."

"Let me see her," the doctor said, and he held Shana to examine her.

Shana hollered all the louder. "Whew, she has good lungs!" the doctor exclaimed. He held Shana for a long time before he said, "I see what you mean. She seems to be in her own world. I'll make an appointment with a specialist at Akron Children's Hospital. Does that sound good to you?"

"Yes, if that is what you think is best for her," Orpha answered as the doctor handed Shana back to her.

Paul and Orpha went to see the specialist the next day. The specialist prescribed a medication he thought would calm Shana and reduce the fussy spells. The medication made the baby sleep, but when she awoke, she was as fussy as ever.

The doctors ordered tests. All the test results came back clear, so after five days Paul and Orpha left the specialist's office and went home without a diagnosis. There was no genetic problem, no blood disorder—no visible signs of any specific syndrome were found. Just a little fussy girl who wasn't developing properly. But was this God's plan?

Orpha began taking Shana for weekly visits to

an osteopathic doctor. Dr. Eberly had a special place in his heart for Shana. He gave his little patient meticulous treatment. Shana loved it so much that the treatments often resulted in the best nap she had for a week.

On one such visit, Dr. Eberly became alarmed. Shana had been crying all night and now, in desperation, Orpha had brought her in for help. Upon further examination, Dr. Eberly detected blood in Shana's stool. He called a specialist at Cleveland University Hospital and had Paul and Orpha make the two-hour trip to see this specialist immediately. Shana screamed heart-wrenching cries all the way to the hospital. By the time she was finally quieted, she had been crying for nineteen hours straight.

Shana's jaw had somehow been dislocated, and she wouldn't nurse anymore. Orpha had to feed Shana with an eyedropper.

When the family got to the hospital, the doctor on duty spent considerable time observing Shana's movements. He told Paul and Orpha, "I think she is on the wrong kind of medication, but I need to talk to my superior before I switch it." The doctor left the room.

Soon he returned and explained that his superior agreed to change medications. When the new drug starting taking effect, it did wonders. Shana stopped tossing from side to side, as she had been doing before. She seemed like a new baby! She was also put on a high-protein supplement to help her gain weight.

Shana spent five days at Cleveland University Hospital, and during this time the doctors did extensive testing. They strapped her hands to the bed to prevent any interference with her jaw realigning. The hospital staff carefully monitored her weight. They discussed putting in a stomach tube, but by the end of five days she had gained enough weight not to need it. That was a big relief to her parents.

Life returned to normal—a new normal. Shana actually seemed to enjoy life. Although she never developed past rolling over and putting her pacifier into her mouth, she did learn to smile and laugh. Shana still had crying spells, but they were not as severe as before.

When Shana was three years old, she became very sick. Orpha took the little girl to a doctor who prescribed strong antibiotics for Shana. Still her fever climbed. The only thing that brought the fever down was sponging her with cool water, and even then, Shana's temperature was far above normal. For two nights she didn't sleep at all. The third evening her fever climbed to 105°. Paul and Orpha took turns sponging their daughter. They prayed in desperation, their strength almost gone. Finally, around eleven o'clock, Shana fell asleep. Orpha lay on the floor beside Shana's crib so she would hear if Shana woke up.

At four-thirty in the morning, Paul awoke with a start, confused. Then he sensed God prompting him to check on Shana. Paul stumbled over to the little crib where his sweet little daughter lay. He could hear that her breathing had changed. He picked Shana up and held her in his arms. She was as limp as a rag doll.

Paul whispered, "Honey, please wake up, I think Shana's in a coma." Orpha awoke with a start and reached for her husband and their precious daughter. They stood like that, arms around each other, for a long time. Tears of sadness crept down their cheeks and spilled onto the rug below.

"Here, dear, you hold her," Paul said at last. "I need to go wake the children."

Orpha wrapped her arms around her little girl and rocked her gently.

Paul quickly headed upstairs and entered his daughter Julia's room. "Julia, wake up if you want to see Shana one last time before she dies." Julia sleepily sat up, confused. Surely this couldn't be real. But it must be, because she saw her daddy carrying Anthony with Jeremy and André in tow.

The little entourage crowded into the nursery to kiss Shana goodbye one last time. They were all crying. Shana was a part of their family! Now she was leaving. What terrible pain was in their hearts.

Shana's breaths became further and further apart. At last she stopped breathing. Shana was gone, never to return. The family stood weeping. It was Monday morning, the beginning of a new week. At that moment, there was nothing they would rather have done than to leave everything and go with her.

Being left behind while watching a loved one leave this world is a pain like no other.

God spoke to Paul through Shana's death. "Someday, when Jesus comes back, there will be many left behind with no hope."

In Matthew 24, Jesus says, "So shall also the coming of the Son of man be. Then shall two be in the field; the one shall be taken, and the other left. Two women shall be grinding at the mill; the one shall be taken, and the other left. Watch therefore: for ye know not what hour your Lord doth come. Therefore be ye also ready: for in such an hour as ye think not the Son of man cometh."

Chapter 20
Somewhere Forever

". . . man goeth to his long home . . ."
—Ecclesiastes 12:5

One Sunday afternoon when Paul was playing with his children outside on the front lawn, his pager beeped. The sheriff dispatcher said, "Attention, East Holmes squad personnel. You have a man down on Township Road 352."

"Oh, that's our neighbor," Paul cried as he ran inside to get his keys. His three oldest children came running behind him. They all jumped into Paul's pickup and rushed to the scene.

This neighbor man was a dear friend of Paul's who loved the Lord. As Paul drove into the driveway, he noticed a pickup parked by the workshop. Paul grabbed his medical bag and jumped out of the truck. He ran through the open door of the workshop. There on the floor lay his neighbor, his friend! Blood oozed from a gash on the man's head. Paul shook him and said, "Dan! Dan!" There was no response.

This was not the Dan Paul knew. Dan had always talked to Paul whenever they met. Now Dan was silent. What had happened? Dan's body was there, but his spirit had gone somewhere else, forever.

xxxxx

On another night Paul was sleeping when his pager beeped. "Attention, East Holmes squad personnel. There's an unresponsive male on Township Road 310."

Paul quickly jumped out of bed and got dressed. He radioed the sheriff's office and said, "Central, dispatch 847 is going direct to scene."

"Copy 847, going direct."

Paul's little truck lurched as it roared out of the driveway. A few minutes later he drove into Tom's driveway. Paul could hear a woman screaming inside the house even before he entered. As Paul opened the door, he heard her say in relief, "Oh, here they are now!"

"Where is he?" Paul asked.

Crying hysterically, the woman pointed down the hallway. "In the bedroom."

Paul ran into the bedroom and there on the water bed lay a tall man. Paul shouted, "Tom, can you hear me?" Tom didn't answer.

Paul grabbed Tom's hand and tried to find a pulse, but couldn't find one. He saw Tom was turning blue. Quickly he radioed the dispatch office. "This is 847. We've got a code blue."

"We copy, 847."

Paul muscled Tom off the bed and onto the floor and began doing CPR. Within minutes the rest of the squad team was there to help. Together they lifted Tom onto a stretcher and rushed him to the hospital. On the way, they attached a heart monitor to Tom. There was no sign of life.

Paul asked again, "Tom, are you with us? Can you tell us where you are, Tom?" Paul suspected Tom was gone, but the squad team worked furiously. Finally, after shocking his heart several times, they got a heartbeat.

When the ambulance arrived at the hospital's emergency room, the doctors were ready and waiting. Tom's heart had started pumping blood again. Maybe, just maybe, he would return to life!

But Tom did not come back. Tom was dead.

Tom had divorced his first wife and married another. He was a man who knew about God. He knew what the Bible says about this kind of adulterous living, but he didn't seem to care.

The lady with whom he lived said, "I went to bed around eleven o'clock. Tom was downstairs watching his favorite television show. I fell asleep and didn't realize when Tom came to bed. Then at around three o'clock in the morning he started making a funny noise. That's when I called 911."

Many people have never heard of Tom. Even those who did know him no longer think of him every day. But Tom is living somewhere forever!

xxxxx

One day while Paul was still working as a refrigeration technician, he was called to work on a cooling system at a house in town. The client,

Steve Carter, came to the door and told Paul where the air conditioner was located. Paul noticed that Steve looked rather sickly, and after fixing the air conditioner he found out why.

"You may have noticed that I'm a sick man. I've been battling cancer and it is slowly wearing me out," Steve said, looking at Paul through tired, sunken eyes.

"I'm sorry to hear that," Paul replied. "Sometimes we don't understand the ways of God. But one thing I do know, God understands every struggle we are going through and He can help us every step of the way."

"Well, I suppose He might," Steve replied.

"I became a Christian when I was a teenager, and God has changed my life," Paul said. "He has been my best friend, especially when I've gone through rough times like you are facing right now."

Steve sighed and said, "I really respect your beliefs and I want what you have. I really do!" He nodded his head. "Could we talk about this later?"

"Yes," agreed Paul, "whenever you are ready."

"Thank you so much for coming out here and blessing my day," Steve said as he closed the door.

"Anytime, and I will be praying for you!" Paul turned and walked down the steps toward his van. He felt heavy inside. Steve seemed so close to the kingdom of God.

As Paul drove back to the shop, he prayed, "God, please give me another chance to talk to Steve before he dies. Bring him to the end of himself and help him see his desperate need of you."

Paul often prayed for Steve Carter during the next few months. Exactly three months later, Paul was called out to Steve's home for a service call again. This time Steve didn't meet Paul at the door. Instead, he lay on a hospital bed in the house, pale and gaunt. Before Paul returned to the shop, he sat down beside the bed and said, "Steve, I remember the conversation we had the last time I was here. Do you remember?"

"Yes, I do," Steve replied. "I really want to talk about my life; I need to change. Maybe later. Yes, later, not today."

"Well, that's fine if you want to talk later," Paul said softly, "but would you mind if I prayed for you before I go?"

"No, go right ahead. I would love that," Steve said, closing his eyes.

"Heavenly Father, you are looking down right now. You see Steve. You see the pain and turmoil his cancer has caused him. Would you be with him and help him? May he find you before he takes his final breath. Give him grace for the trial he is going through, and may he find hope in you, O Lord. We pray this in your precious name, Amen."

With tears in his eyes, Steve bade Paul goodbye.

As Paul walked down the steps toward his van, he felt a heavy burden on his heart. Oh, how sad Steve's situation was! Steve looked so forlorn, so lost and forsaken. How God could change his life! *Why do we delay,* Paul wondered to himself as he turned onto Main Street, *when there is mercy today, and love and peace like none other? O God, speak to*

Steve's heart.

The very next day, Paul got word that Steve Carter had died. Steve is now somewhere forever. Steve wanted to change later, but he had waited too long.

xxxxx

"Now is the day of salvation" (2 Corinthians 6:2b).

Hebrews 9:27 says, "It is appointed unto men once to die, but after this the judgment."

James 4:14 says, "Whereas ye know not what shall be on the morrow. For what is your life? It is even a vapour, that appeareth for a little time, and then vanisheth away."

Matthew 25:31-34, 41 depicts a scene that we all will face someday. "When the Son of man shall come in his glory, and all the holy angels with him, then shall he sit upon the throne of his glory: And before him shall be gathered all nations: and he shall separate them one from another, as a shepherd divideth his sheep from the goats: And he shall set the sheep on his right hand, but the goats on the left. Then shall the king say unto them on his right hand, Come, ye blessed of my Father, inherit the kingdom prepared for you from the foundation of the world. Then shall he say also unto them on the left hand, Depart from me, ye cursed, into everlasting fire, prepared for the devil and his angels."

Sometimes life on earth seems like an unending journey, but in reality, it is quite short.

Every human soul will be somewhere forever

after death. *Considering that you could die without warning, as Dan and Tom did, you need to think about your eternal destiny.*

Have you ever wondered how it will be like to be somewhere forever? How long is forever? If forever were a trillion years, how long would that be? A million seconds ago was twelve days ago. A billion seconds ago was thirty years ago. And a trillion seconds ago was thirty thousand years ago, long before the earth and time were created. When we've lived a trillion years, the next trillion years have just begun. Forever is a long, long time!

Note to the Reader

At the time of this writing, Paul Weaver is an ordained deacon and pastor at Still Waters Mennonite Church of Jackson, Ohio. He is also assistant director of Christian Aid Ministries. Paul and Orpha have one daughter and three sons. Julia, the author of this book, lives in Michigan with her husband, Lawrence, and their three young sons. Jeremy is married to Jennifer, and André and Anthony still live at home.

As you read about some of Paul's important experiences, his desire is that you will find the heavenly Father he loves and be strengthened in your faith. His great concern is that God is seen and glorified in this book. Though he went through months of fear and turmoil before he surrendered to God, and though he experienced miracles and heavenly visits, he does not want Christians who haven't had such experiences to begin pursuing miraculous signs or doubt their standing with God. God works in many ways in different lives. The important thing is to be born again and fully surrendered to Him.

The following words are displayed in Paul's office and reflect his utmost desire:

My deepest regret:
That I have only one life to give
to the service of God.

Julia enjoys hearing from readers and can be contacted by e-mail at jpwcricket@juno.com or written to in care of Christian Aid Ministries, P.O. Box 360, Berlin, Ohio, 44610.

About Christian Aid Ministries

Christian Aid Ministries was founded in 1981 as a nonprofit, tax-exempt 501(c)(3) organization. Its primary purpose is to provide a trustworthy and efficient channel for Amish, Mennonite, and other conservative Anabaptist groups and individuals to minister to physical and spiritual needs around the world. This is in response to the command ". . . do good unto all men, especially unto them who are of the household of faith" (Gal. 6:10).

Each year, CAM supporters provide approximately 15 million pounds of food, clothing, medicines, seeds, Bibles, Bible story books, and other Christian literature for needy people. Most of the aid goes to orphans and Christian families. Supporters' funds also help clean up and rebuild for natural disaster victims, put up Gospel billboards in the U.S., support several church-planting efforts, operate two medical clinics, and provide resources for needy families to make their own living. CAM's main purposes for providing aid are to help and encourage God's people and bring the Gospel to a lost and dying world.

CAM has staff, warehouse, and distribution networks in Romania, Moldova, Ukraine, Haiti, Nicaragua, Liberia, and Israel. Aside from management, supervisory personnel, and bookkeeping operations, volunteers do most of the work at CAM locations. Each year, volunteers at our warehouses, field bases, DRS projects, and other locations donate over 200,000 hours of work.

CAM's ultimate purpose is to glorify God and help enlarge His kingdom. ". . . whatsoever ye do, do all to the glory of God" (I Cor. 10:31).

Steps to Salvation

The Bible says that we all have "sinned and come short of the glory of God" (Romans 3:23). We sin because we give heed to our sinful nature inherited from Adam's sin in the Garden of Eden, and our sin separates us from God.

God provided the way back to Himself by His only Son, Jesus Christ, who became the spotless Lamb "slain from the foundation of the world." "For God so loved the world that he gave his only begotten Son, that whosoever believeth in him should not perish, but have everlasting life" (John 3:16).

To be reconciled to God and experience life rather than death, and heaven rather than hell (Deuteronomy 30:19), we must repent and believe in the Son of God, the Lord Jesus Christ (Romans 6:32; 6:16).

When we sincerely repent of our sins (Acts 2:38; 3:19; 17:30) and by faith receive Jesus Christ as our Saviour and Lord, God saves us by His grace and we are born again. "That if thou shalt confess with thy mouth the Lord Jesus, and shalt believe in thine heart that God hath raised him from the dead, thou shalt be saved" (Romans 10:9). "For by grace are ye saved through faith; and that not of yourselves: it is the gift of God" (Ephesians 2:8).

When we become born again in Jesus Christ, we become new creatures (2 Corinthians 5:17). We do not continue in sin (1 John 3:9), but give testimony of our new life in Jesus Christ by baptism and obedience to Him. "He that hath my commandments, and keepeth them, he it is that loveth me: and he that loveth me shall be loved of my Father, and I will love him, and will manifest myself to him" (John 14:21).

To grow spiritually, we need to meditate on God's Word and commune with God in prayer. Fellowship with a faithful group of believers is also important to strengthen and maintain our Christian walk (1 John 1:7).